TRAVELS
IN
MANCHURIA AND MONGOLIA

TRAVELS IN MANCHURIA AND MONGOLIA

A Feminist Poet from Japan Encounters Prewar China

Yosano Akiko

TRANSLATED BY JOSHUA A. FOGEL

COLUMBIA UNIVERSITY PRESS

NEW YORK

Columbia University Press

Publishers Since 1893

New York   Chichester, West Sussex

Copyright © 2001 Columbia University Press

Library of Congress Cataloging-in-Publication Data

Yosano, Akiko, 1848–1942.

[Man-Mo yuki. English]

Travels in Manchuria and Mongolia / Yosano Akiko ; translated and edited by

Joshua A. Fogel.

p.   cm.

Includes bibliographical references and index.

ISBN 0-231-12318-3 (cloth : alk. paper)—ISBN 0-231-12319-1 (pbk. : alk. paper)

1. Yosano, Akiko, 1848–1942—Journeys—China—Manchuria.   2. Yosano, Akiko,

1848–1942—Journeys—Mongolia.   3. Manchuria (China)—Description and

travel.   4. Mongolia—Description and travel.   I. Fogel, Joshua A., 1950–

II. Title.

PL819.O8 M3613 2001

895.6'84403—dc21

[B]   2001028015

CIP

Casebound editions of Columbia University Press books are printed on permanent

and durable acid-free paper.

Designed by Chang Jae Lee

Printed in the United States of America

c 10 9 8 7 6 5 4 3 2 1

p 10 9 8 7 6 5 4 3 2 1

CONTENTS

ACKNOWLEDGMENTS

It behooves me to acknowledge the assistance of two people in the translation of this text. My colleague Toshi Hasegawa helped me go over spots I had found problematic throughout the travelogue, and Christopher Atwood was kind enough to answer an endless string of queries about Mongolian references in the text that I would never have been able to decipher without his help. Finally, Janine Beichman, who has worked extensively on Yosano Akiko, was kind enough to read through the introduction and make numerous helpful suggestions. Unless otherwise noted, all poems within the travelogue were originally written in Japanese.

TRAVELS
IN
MANCHURIA AND MONGOLIA

YOSANO AKIKO
AND
HER CHINA TRAVELOGUE OF 1928

Joshua A. Fogel

Yosano Akiko (1878–1942) was one of Japan's greatest poets and translators from classical Japanese. Born into a confection shopkeeper's home in the city of Sakai outside Osaka, she had the good fortune, despite her gender, of being reared in a household full of books. Although her father banished her at the age of one month to the home of an aunt because he so wanted another son, she returned to her natal home after the birth of her brother in August 1880, when she was twenty months old. While she bore the many responsibilities for minding the shop, she consumed the classics of Japanese literature. At the Sakai Girls' High School from which she graduated in 1895, she continued reading broadly in Japanese literature as well as European literature and poetry, though most of this must have been done on her own given the level of pedagogy at the time at such a school. In September 1895 when she was a mere sixteen years of age, she published her maiden poem, in the tanka style, in *Bungei kurabu* (Literary Club), a journal in Tokyo.

In August 1900 she met the famed poet Yosano Tekkan (Hiroshi, 1873–1935) who was the effective leader of the romantic movement in contemporary Japanese poetry. Although he was married at the time, that common law marriage was on the rocks. Akiko soon thereafter, in June 1901, ran off to Tokyo to live with him, and they were married that September. For the next few years, Akiko published her poetry in Tekkan's well-known journal, *Myōjō* (Bright Star), and she helped him edit the journal until its demise in 1908—as well as during its return to publication from 1921 to 1927. Her first volume of poems, *Midaregami* (Tangled Hair), containing some four hundred poems, was also published in 1901. This collection was brimming with passion and sensuality, a courageous enough project for a man at the time, let alone for a young woman.

Her eventual output was extraordinary, including over twenty volumes of poetry and a widely used translation of the ancient classic, *The Tale of Genji*, into modern Japanese. In a Japanese rendition of *A Star Is Born*, just as Akiko's reputation began to soar, Tekkan's was veering into a steady decline. It would be an exaggeration to say that his career was defunct by this point, but during their marriage and rearing of eleven children, it would be the sales of her books that kept the Yosano clan afloat.

In November 1911 Tekkan set sail for a long trip to France. Akiko joined him in May of the following year, coming by rail across Northeast Asia and the Trans-Siberian Railway, a trip to which she alludes in the 1928 travelogue translated herein. In France and elsewhere in Western Europe, the Yosanos met with well-known writers and artists with whom they shared aesthetic as well as social concerns. It was during this second decade of the twentieth century that Akiko was becoming increasingly aware of the social problems of Taishō-era Japan, and especially of the needs of Japanese women. The experiences in Europe reenforced this awareness.

Yosano Akiko is particularly celebrated for her contributions to Japan's first feminist journal of creative writing, *Seitō* (Blue Stocking). She grew to be an outspoken proponent of women's education and suffrage, and in 1921 she became dean and professor at Bunka Gakuin, a free coeducational school, which she founded together with her husband and others. She remained open throughout her life, despite the rigors of raising so many children and fulfilling her many obligations, to meeting younger talents, particularly younger women, in the world of poetry.

When Akiko was at the peak of her career, she and her husband received an offer from the South Manchurian Railway Company (SMR) to sponsor them on a trip through Northeast Asia. Their departure for Manchuria in the spring of 1928 was widely publicized throughout the region, as the extraordinary reception they received everywhere along the route of their travels demonstrates. The late 1920s were a high point of Sino-Japanese tensions, as the Japanese civil and military expansion into Manchuria and North China proceeded. Indeed, the Yosanos had planned to travel south to Beijing, but they were advised against it because of potential violence erupting in that city. On several occasions they directly witnessed anti-Japanese incidents, especially after the murder by Japanese army officers of Manchurian warlord Zhang Zuolin (1875–1928).

The Yosanos wrote a joint travelogue comprised of Akiko's narrative of their voyage and the poems of both. Translated here is Akiko's discursive account, which includes inter alia a number of her husband's poems, some in Chinese and some in Japanese. There is considerable evidence—in the form of numerous classical Chinese references to poetic and prose texts—

that she did extensive research about China either before or, more likely, afterward. The inclusion of offhand references to old and often arcane sources or obscure poetry as a way of demonstrating the author's familiarity with traditional Chinese culture was already by this time a well-trod path for Japanese visitors to China who wrote travelogues. Clearly, even someone with a photographic memory could not have had at his or her fingertips such an enormous breadth of learning—and no Japanese carried the necessary dozens of Chinese texts with them in China.

Akiko was by no means the first Japanese to have his or her trip completely funded by the SMR. That honor fell to Natsume Sōseki (1867–1916) in 1909, and the success of that joint venture led to SMR sponsorship of other celebrated writers over the years. Sōseki was well aware of the potentially comprising position in which he found himself: traveling through Manchuria on the SMR lines with the SMR funding the entire trip and hoping to come to objective conclusions about the activities of Japanese enterprises in the region. He actually confronted the dilemma directly, self-mockingly, and then dismissed it. By contrast, Yosano Akiko never once mentions that all the extraordinary courtesies she and her husband received during their weeks in Manchuria and Mongolia might in any way influence what she was writing about Japanese activities there.

Countless Japanese travelogues of China had been written over the previous two or three decades, newspapers had correspondents filing regular reports from numerous Chinese cities, Japan had an embassy and numerous consulates throughout the land, there were Japanese communities in many Chinese cities, and because of the Sino-Japanese War of 1894–95 many Japanese had already seen the real China. By 1928, in addition to

Sōseki, Futabatei Shimei (1864–1909), Kawahigashi Hekigotō (1873–1937), Ōmachi Keigetsu (1869–1925), Tayama Katai (1871–1930), Akutagawa Ryūnosuke (1892–1927), Tanizaki Jun'ichirō (1886–1965), Satō Haruo (1892–1964), and many other writers and poets had traveled through China and written travel narratives.[1] Tanigawa, Akutagawa, and Satō, for example, met extensively with Chinese intellectuals and writers. By 1928, though, with Sino-Japanese tensions high, that experience all but vanishes from Akiko's realm of possibilities. By the time Akiko visited the Asian mainland, contemporary China was a known commodity back in Japan, but the Chinese were becoming less willing to be a part of Japanese travel accounts.

In order to appeal to her readership back home, Akiko had to fashion a travel narrative that reflected both her pressing creative needs and her distinctive responses to the fascinating but often tense worlds in which she traveled in Manchuria and Mongolia. What then makes Akiko's travel narrative distinctive? The answer to this important question has more to do with Akiko's fame as a poet in her day and less with her critical perceptiveness about China and the Chinese. Interestingly, Akiko's travelogue of China has little poetic about it, save the poems included in the text that she and her husband penned en route. Instead, it offers marvelous descriptions of peoples and places and displays a rich vocabulary that is often challenging to the translator. Especially in Mongolia, her descriptions go into great detail, with, for example, precise measurements of a model yurt. Elsewhere, as well, she is always precise about dates, time of day, distances between two sites, foods consumed and their cost, and those present at every meeting.

Having said all this, it should be noted that, unlike Tanizaki and others before her, Akiko met with few Chinese and with not a single Chinese writer or poet. There were Japanese-speaking

Chinese guides at several places and a prolonged, lovely meeting with the wives of two Chinese warlords. Otherwise her encounters in Manchuria were exclusively with other Japanese—innkeepers, businessmen and their wives, and especially the many employees of the South Manchurian Railway Company and their wives. The Yosanos also met with a number of Japanese they had known from earlier associations in Japan or through mutual friends, as China was becoming a meeting place for Japanese away from home. Not only does this reveal the great numbers of Japanese living in the region but it also gives us considerable insight into the relative insularity of the Japanese community on the mainland.

China, Manchuria, Mongolia—in the form of their mountains, their temples and shrines, their natural beauty, their cities and throughfares—are there to be seen, but only rarely interacted with. At one point, Akiko stresses that, for all their study of things Chinese, Japanese of the Edo period (1600–1868) could not really have *understood* it, because they could never have *seen* it. Understanding China, thus, comes only after it has become the object of an outside gaze—after it has been experienced. What this *experience* entails, however, remains extremely vague. It clearly does not necessitate significant engagement with the local populace but can apparently be gleaned simply through the visual gaze. Akiko definitely wants to experience this foreign reality herself, but she never penetrates beyond the scenery, its historical and poetic resonances, and the appearances of the Chinese and other ethnic groups encountered en route. At the same time, Japan appears to remain the only reality that has meaning for her and enables her to gain peace and serenity or overcome loneliness; with a few exceptions, it is only when she meets other Japanese in China that she finds composure. It is telling that when she sets out to buy souvenirs for her daughters back home in Japan, she goes to the famed

Churin Department Store and purchases European trinkets, not Chinese ones. Perhaps Chinese items would not have been exotic enough or not worthy of the stature they were to receive in her travel narrative. Perhaps she simply knew in advance what her children would want.

Hence, the *Man-Mō yūki* translated here for the first time into English has only incidental insights to offer us about China and the Chinese. It is much more valuable as a document for the study of Japanese representations of China and for the study of Yosano Akiko herself. Although she clearly states her sympathies for the sufferings of the Chinese people and is upset by the movements of Japanese troops occasioned by the murder of Zhang Zuolin, she does not share these sentiments directly with any Chinese. In her narrative, then, the Chinese emerge as an extremely hardworking people, suffering under great pressures and internal disunion. China emerges as a country of great natural beauty, which time and human despoliation have not completely ruined. China also emerges as a site for her to meet many, many Japanese.

For all her feminism, Yosano never became a radical political activist. She remained a liberal in her era, and the virtual absence of Chinese voices in her travelogue is as well an indication of her edginess with respect to the world she was visiting and, perhaps, reveals something of a fear of China itself. While she was aware and, indeed, critical of Japanese imperialism in its uglier militarist guises, she was only too happy to be protected by Japanese troops when the situation became potentially violent. Interestingly, she never questions this contradiction. She is even willing to commend Chinese nationalism as a potential sign of a better future for China, but when it manifests itself in an unpleasant way—such as in the behavior of Zhang Huanxiang, a local military leader, in Harbin—she becomes irritated, and nationalism becomes, in her estimation, xenophobia. This disjunction is by no means unique in Akiko's response to China at this time. Many Japanese of a liberal bent fell into a similar trap.

By the same token, China and the Chinese did not speak in a single unitary voice. For all the overdetermined scholarship on Chinese nationalism, there were many, often contradictory, manifestations of modern nationalism in China of the 1920s and 1930s, and there was a significant group of Chinese sympathetic to Japan. Even the pro-Japanese types, however, escaped Akiko's purview. Her travelogue, then, remains a much more personal, intimate portrait of China and the Chinese. And, it thus is full of ambiguities, both exhilaration and unease, enjoyment and fear. There is, of course, no ideal Platonic travelogue to which all real ones may be compared, and all travelogues are personal documents, even those proclaiming to be a documentary account of the land and people visited. One of the great strengths of Yosano Akiko's travel narrative is the tension brewing beneath the surface, the ambiguities, and even the self-deception of one who travels around in a sedan chair, expecting to get a sense of the real people and their feelings.

TRAVELS

IN

MANCHURIA AND MONGOLIA

Yosano Akiko

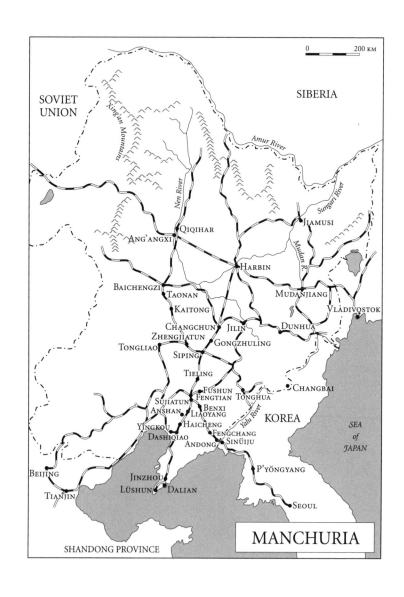

SOVIET
UNION

SIBERIA

Xing'an Mountains

Amur River

Nen River

Sungari River

QIQIHAR

JIAMUSI

ANG'ANGXI

HARBIN

Mudan R.

BAICHENGZI

TAONAN

MUDANJIANG

KAITONG

VLADIVOSTOK

CHANGCHUN   JILIN

DUNHUA

ZHENGJIATUN   GONGZHULING

TONGLIAO

SIPING

TIELING

FUSHUN

CHANGBAI

SUJIATUN   FENGTIAN   TONGHUA

ANSHAN   BENXI

LIAOYANG

YINGKOU   HAICHENG

Yalu River

KOREA

DASHIQIAO   FENGCHANG

ANDONG   SINŬIJU

SEA
of
JAPAN

BEIJING

P'YŎNGYANG

JINZHOU

TIANJIN

LÜSHUN   DALIAN

SEOUL

SHANDONG PROVINCE

MANCHURIA

0   200 KM

On the morning of the sixteenth [of May 1928], Mr. Katō Ikuya, my husband, and I boarded an express train on the main line of the South Manchurian Railway and departed from Dalian. Messrs. Usami, Kohiyama, Ishikawa, Mayama, Nishida, and their wives, among many others, came to send us off from the Dalian Station.

When we arrived at the Jinzhou Station, the stationmaster was kind enough to provide us with a young Chinese railway porter who could speak Japanese as our guide. We all boarded a horse-drawn coach and set out first to visit battlefields of the Sino-Japanese and Russo-Japanese Wars in nearby Nanshan.[1] Nanshan, or "southern mountain," was low-lying hilly terrain, a part of the Jinzhou plain. There amid some young pine trees had been erected a white granite commemorative tablet. While paying our condolences on the battlefield, it was refreshing to look at the wide-open green field where the sorghum had just come into bloom in the clear May sky. I spotted "dandelions" and wild "irises" sprouting in disarray, and when my husband asked what their Chinese names were, the young railway porter told us that "iris" in Chinese was *yanziyi* and "dandelion" was *popoding*. The name *yanzihua* for the fully bloomed flower of the iris was an elegant Chinese name since antiquity and was even known in Japan, but *yanziyi*—literally, the wing of the swallow—was a provincialism I was hearing for the first time. My husband was even more pleased by the name *popoding*. The *ding* was a term added to the names of scented flowers, such as *dingzihua* (clove), *chending* (aloes), *zidingxiang* (lilac). He noted that it might be shown that the Japanese word for dandelion— *tanpopo*—was an ancient Chinese term in which *ding* represented the first character [i.e., *tan*].

JINZHOU

As we left Nanshan, the natural scenery of the road en route to the city of Jinzhou afforded us great pleasure. From the midst of the riverside willows that followed the road, the city walls of Jinzhou in front of a green field and the charming watchtower above them appeared like a chart of the palace of the dragon king. Chinese carts of various and sundry shapes passed one another along the road, and the carefree manner in which we moved among them in the horse-drawn coach had, save for the clouds of white dust they raised, a fascinating charm for us in this foreign land.

We passed through the gate of the city into Jinzhou, and there for the first time I saw the Chinese city encircled by the city walls. One can really see how different the Chinese term for "city" (*cheng*) is from the Japanese conception of that same term, pronounced *shiro* [meaning "castle" or "castle town"].

This was a city that had taken shape on the site of the ancient capital of Liaodong. The bustling scene seemed to be limited to the central street, although opulent merchant homes and massive residences of the elite formed a thick wall along a side road. My husband wrote down his impressions of this central street in his diary as follows:

> Rising clouds of white dust, a stench seemingly caused by food, the shadows and cacophony of men and horses. The pavement was sunken with wheel ruts. Merchants selling furniture with glimmering cast iron fixtures, restaurants, stables, apothecaries. In the midst of it all, a strangely oversized dark red coffin at a funeral items shop and accessories in animal form appearing rather ostentatious. Right in the middle of the street, an obese black and white mottled pig was being

carried alive by two able-bodied men who were weighing and bargaining over it. The pale blue clothing of city people who surrounded this scene looking on at leisure was thoroughly soiled and stained to the point of being black, reflecting white in the sunlight.

One of the public schools that had been established at various sites by the South Manchurian Railway Company for the education of the Chinese was outside the city walls of Jinzhou. We visited a certain Japanese teacher at this public school, and he took us to see the famed Tianqi Shrine outside the eastern wall. The Chinese word for "shrine" (*miao*) contrasts with a "temple" (*si*). They use the term *miao* for shrines large and small alike. In recent times, Daoist shrines have proliferated and to a certain extent become mixed with Buddhist ones. Tianqi is a Daoist deity, the principal deity of Mount Tai in Shandong province. We heard that there are many such Tianqi shrines scattered about Manchuria where, for many years past, Han Chinese from Shandong have been settling.

The Tianqi Shrine here in Jinzhou, however, was now a Chan Buddhist temple of the Yunxi sect. It is now inhabited not by Daoist priests but by Buddhist monks who supervise its maintenance. The shrine is divided into a main hall and residential quarters; the latter can be found in the back where images of husband and wife deities are dressed in ordinary garb. The day was peaceful, and it seemed as though, having forgotten all duties to heaven, man, and earth, these deities were immersed in the tranquillity and joy of family. To the left and right, four bodhisattvas were standing, each with one item raised: a work of literature, an inkstone, a *pipa*, and a *qin*.[2] It appeared as though these were images of deities appropriately drawn from a "country of rites and music." There may be no other country in which among a group of religious images one finds husband and wife deities symbolizing the transformation of family life by learning and scholarship.

The shrine is also famous for the sculptures located in a detached hall depicting various aspects of hell. Although these are works of the Qing era [1644–1911] of no particular artistic value, there was one of ironic design: a human being getting weighed, having the severity of his crimes calculated, and, in order to end the sufferings in hell and clothe the soul that would be released, the skins of various animals were carved, among them one human skin. The creation of such sculpture and paintings as an aide in exhortations to belief is a rather old Buddhist technique. We find them as early as in the poems of hungry spirits in the *Man'yōshû* [Collection of Ten Thousand Leaves, compiled eighth century] as well as in the sculptures contained in the pagoda of the Hōryūji, but in present-day Liaodong, too, one can find instructive reference.

In recent years past, from the earth on these grounds a discovery by scholars who have brought to light a stele bearing an inscription concerning the Mongol invasion during the Kōan period [1278–88] has already been reported among Japanese historians. This stele is preserved in the Nanjing School that sits in a Confucian temple in Jinzhou. We went to this temple and were able to read the inscription itself. Although this temple was in a dilapidated state, vestiges of the ancient style of its architecture remained in its garden and pond.

The land near Jinzhou was of a curiously light reddish hue on the whole. There was also soil of a much deeper red. This redness continued as far as the sands of the river bed. The beauti-

8

ful, gentle scenery that was reflected in the fresh verdure of the willow trees extended as far as our field of vision—a picturesque scene such as cannot be found in Japan. Although the scenery of south China is surely magnificent, the color of the earth there is probably not the red one finds here in Jinzhou. The willow catkins not yet to be found in Dalian during this season had already scattered and piled up here and there upon our arrival in Jinzhou. The flower blossoms like cotton or the fluffy down on a baby's cheek wafted lightly and quietly in the faint gentle breeze. No, these were not blossoms, but the cottonlike substance that comes out of the blossoms. Had the strength of the wind increased even slightly, they would have whirled up into the sky and flown off to some distant place, who knows where. This truly harmonizes with the atmosphere under the crystal clear, blue sky of Manchuria, which gets so little rain, with its aroma of late spring, early summer sun and fresh leaves—it all renders the mind graceful and lucid. Sweeping over the cart in which we were traveling, they scattered about us repeatedly. We were so happy to be able to see for the first time here those things known as willow catkins (*liuxu* or *yanghua*) in Chinese literature. My husband cited a poem by Wu Rong, a poet from the Tang period (618–907), and then said, "I now understand the joy of this poem. Somehow the willow catkins seem to love the wind, and they seem to be loved by it." I penned the poem that follows:

That day, south of the city, riding in the horse-drawn cart with the teacher from Jinzhou, the willow catkins scattered over us.

XIONGYUECHENG

After spending half a day seeing Jinzhou, we left by train in the afternoon, heading for Xiongyuecheng Station. Above the low mountain range visible through the window on the right side of the train, we saw a "smoke platform" from the Ming dynasty [1368–1644] built of piled stone that had partially collapsed, though remains could be seen here and there. It was a signaling station that had been created in the face of invading Japanese pirates.

The station was only a few miles from the city of Xiong-yuecheng. Guided here as well, this time by the director of the local public school, we first paid a call by car on the Agricul-tural Experimentation Station operated by the South Manchur-ian Railway. After listening to gracious explanations by the staff and inspecting various reference specimens of their work, we were able to get a general conception of the produce dis-tinctive to northern and southern Manchuria. I am ordinarily not much interested in statistics, but I sensed that the numbers were very useful in developing such a general concept.

From there we went on to sightseeing in the streets of Xiongyuecheng, the local capital. The city walls face the right bank of the Xiongyue River. Because this area, unlike Jinzhou, was outside Japanese leased territory, we requested the permis-sion of the Chinese police and climbed the watchtower of the eastern wall. While walking along the ramparts, with the river in front of us, we looked out onto the plains to the south and the mountains to the northeast. The breadth of the city walls was quite expansive, twelve feet wide. There were many rivers in Manchuria bearing the name *shahe* [lit. "sand river"], and, as the name indicates, these were usually rivers of sand; shortly after a rainfall, water would appear, but as we looked at the Xiong-yue River today only a trickling of water was passing through.

Standing before the great river that pours into the Gulf of Zhili while gazing at the mountains on the other bank of the river, that is a scene from bygone days befitting a trip to China. Inside the city, the YMCA was proselytzing the anti-Japanese cause, and we were warned of the possibility of danger to us. We thus speedily passed through the hook-shaped main street from the eastern wall to the northern. Like Jinzhou, the main street here was alive and bustling with shops and restaurants. White dust clouds were dense and a certain smell was mixed into all manner of items; I covered my face with a handkerchief and we pressed on. We were about to enter a car waiting outside the northern wall, but no Chinese driver appeared. While we waiting, a crowd of people gathered around us. Their eyes were fastened particularly on me, with the Western clothes I was wearing, and because I associated this with anti-Japanese stories that had circulated since the Jinan incident,[3] I had a bit of an ominous sense. After about twenty minutes, the driver appeared, and when I asked him the name of the item he was carrying in his hand, he replied that it was called *zongzi* [rice dumplings wrapped in bamboo leaves], the same item we call *chimaki*. It is triangular in shape, wrapped in a reed leaf, and steamed. They make these *zong* [or *zongzi*] in May just as we do in Japan, a practice that was probably conveyed from southern China in antiquity. We found it extremely interesting that contemporary Chinese in Manchuria also carry on this custom. As my husband wrote:

> The Chinese *zong* folding into a triangle the reed leaf
> from the Xiongyue River in early summer.

We next returned to the Agricultural Experimentation Station, and, with the kind guidance of the agronomists there, we observed specimens of things produced in Manchuria: grains, vegetables, fruits, silk and cotton, and flora and fauna. We also saw the plants and seedlings on a huge farm and were given an object lesson on the spot. There were various sorts of sorghum and over forty different varieties of beans.

That night we stayed at the Xiongyue Hot Springs. Located on the west bank of the upper reaches of the Xiongyue River, the hot springs inn was managed by Japanese. Water from the hot springs was drawn indoors at various points by the sandy source of the river where it was boiling up, and particularly unusual was the fact that the water came from the river's source and one could bathe here freely in the hot water of the sand. Apparently, in the summer Japanese bathers from Dalian and elsewhere flock to this place, while Chinese, whether they are native to the area or passing through, strip, dig in the sand, and have the nearby flow of water poured over them to their hearts' content as they adjust to the water's termperature. They sink down as far as their heads and look up at the nearby mountains beneath the blue sky, carrying on friendly conversation while viewing the forest of willow trees. It is a scene of extraordinary restfulness. That evening, Japanese from the Agricultural Experimentation Station, the public school, and elsewhere, together with their spouses and children, gathered at the inn, and we chatted with them leisurely.

The Xiongyue Hot Springs is rich in mountain, river, and willow scenery, and the quality of the springs is on a par with Hakone in terms of beauty. The starkly bald rocky mountain that juts out nearby has an unusual shape. They call it both Wang'ershan (Watching boy mountain) and Wangxiaoshan (Small watching mountain). The story is told that in olden days a lad traveled to the capital to compete in the civil service examinations; his mother climbed this peak and waited day after day for his return until she finally died of agony. My husband penned the following poem:

Although the mountains we see are all clear, only the mountain looking at the young lad sits in a cold plain. There is a mountain looking out for the boy amid the willow trees of Manchuria, but the eastern capital is far away.

I then recited the following poem:

The mother stood and stared from Wangxiaoshan, they say, her child far away in the capital.

YINGKOU

At Dashiqiao Station on the main line of the South Manchurian Railway, we changed to the Yingkou branch line and arrived at Yingkou. I had wanted to see the estuary of the Liao River, which I knew from history, but, more important, I wanted to see the daughter of Mr. Furusawa—she was my first student at the Bunka Academy, a young woman with an extraodinary temperament, full of literary talent. She had recently married and was there with her husband, Mr. Hayakawa.

Yingkou stood on the left bank of the Liao River estuary. In the late Qing era the government set up a bureaucratic office there known as the Zhenhaiying [lit. "encampment to protect the sea"]. Yingkou was popularly known as Yingzikou.

We were met at the station by the stationmaster as well as by Mr. and Mrs. Matsue. When I gazed upon the healthy and beautiful face of Mrs. Matsue, about whose health I had been concerned, tears of joy and relief welled up in my eyes. I was reticent to speak, and then I blurted out to Mrs. Matsue more than I should have. The ever naïve Mrs. Matsue seemed full of joy, as she quietly was heard to say, "Yes, yes." I have never been in the position of being someone else's teacher, but although I am poorly trained in classical Japanese literature, if there was a certain understanding that I had acquired I simply prayed that I might convey it to three or four older women with whom I had contact. I privately counted Mrs. Matsue among those three or four.

With the stationmaster's kind assistance we boarded the steam launch, and together with Mr. and Mrs. Matsue we traveled several miles up the Liao River. The Liao begins in the Xing'an Mountain Range of Inner Mongolia, and then uniting with rivers at various sites along the way flows some five hundred miles before arriving at Yingkou and entering the Gulf of Zhili. It is, together with the Sungari River, one of the two great rivers of Manchuria and Mongolia. The term *Liaodong* [lit. "east of Liao"] appears for the first time in the biography of a man by the name of Su Qin in the *Shiji* (Records of the Grand Historian) and, in fact, takes its name from this river.[4] The ancient meaning of the term *Liaodong*, according to the research of the author of the *Liaodong wenxian zhenglüe* (Verification in Brief of Documents About Liaodong), was not as narrow as construed in later eras, but was a comprehensive term for a wide area covering from Yuguan (Shanhaiguan) east to all of the present-day Three Eastern Provinces [Manchuria] and the eastern portion of Rehe. Properly speaking, Yingkou is about 34 miles upriver from the estuary, and another mile or more upriver leads to a water depth that during high tide can buoy up a battleship. Chinese junks sail a distance of 179 miles upstream as far as Zhengjiatun in Inner Mongolia, which sits at the upper reaches of three rivers. Calculating the total distance they travel upstream along tributaries would come to about 360 miles. The width of the river before Yingkou is some 250 feet; it is filled with mud and the rushing whirlpool presents a fearful sight. Reeds are growing densely in one area on the far shore of the river, and beyond it lies a plain where the mountains' shadows cannot be seen. There is a railway station for a branch line of the Jing-Feng railway in western Yingkou on the opposite shore; twice a day small steamships from Yingkou link up with the train, making it possible to travel between Beijing and Fengtian.

The stationmaster pointed out and explained numerous things to us on board the steam launch. In the new city near the station, consulates from a number of countries and firms and shops were lined up in an orderly fashion. The Chinese city, known as the Old City, could be seen slightly further downriver. For the first time in my life, I saw junks converging here. They came from Tianjin and Zhifu and, as just described, sailed upstream. Chinese poets of old have compared the cluster of their masts to a forest, and I had the eerie sense that I was seeing just such an image. Once, during a trip to Holland, I enjoyed the beauty of the flags of ships forming a group, but the fluttering red and blue and yellow of the banners on these junks contrasted with the muddy waters beneath the cloudy sky. There was, in fact, a certain grandeur about it all.

According to the stationmaster, in winter the river freezes over, and horse-drawn carts travel over it. Also, innumerable wild geese fly across to the far shore of the river and render it completely black. During the thawing period in spring, ice comes floating down from the upper reaches of the river, making for a magnificent sight. He also noted that there have never been any cases of people who inadvertently fell in this river and reemerged, for while the surface of the river gives the appearance of calm, below it are surging whirlpools.

DASHIQIAO

We noticed that there was a mistake on the train timetable, and the train did not leave at the hour we had expected it would. Mr. Katō, our guide, was worriedly fidgeting, but the stationmaster said to us, "There's a locomotive heading back to Dashiqiao. Go ahead and take it, because it will soon be ready to depart." Resigned to the heat, soot and smoke, and oscillation, we had decided to do so, and the stationmaster found us an empty conductor's car and had it connected to the locomotive for us. With this extraordinary kindness, we boarded our temporary special train, and at peak speed we road back to Daishiqiao Station. Ten minutes after arriving there, we were overjoyed to be able to switch to an express train that had just arrived from Dalian.

On Mizhen Mountain in the environs of Dashiqiao Station stood the ancient Haiyun Temple. On its grounds the Niangniang Shrine for prayer was famous among all similarly named shrines throughout Manchuria, because each year beginning on the sixteenth day of the fourth lunar month numerous women believers gathered from near and far for three days of rituals. *Niangniang* was said to encompass the three female Daoist deities of Yunxiao, Bixiao, and Qiongxiao, and they thus were apportioned, respectively, the functions of prosperity and longevity, correcting eyesight, and the delivery of children. Passing by, we looked up at this shrine that seemed to hang down amid the craggy rocks on the mountainside.

TANGGANGZI AND QIANSHAN

We got off the train at the Tanggangzi Station on the main line of the South Manchurian Railway and put up at a hotel by the Tanggangzi Hot Springs in front of the station. As I was thinking about the local toponyms, such as *Tanggangzi* and nearby *Tanghe* and *Ganquanpu,* I realized that the hot water of the local hot springs must have dated back to ancient times. It was a beautiful alkali spring. The hotel was indirectly managed by the South Manchurian Railway Company, its structure immense in scale and its proprietors scrupulously attentive to conveniences within. We also appreciated that the maids all preserved the humility of respectable young women and had nothing of the air of waitresses about them. We were now on a plain among the willow trees, and, regrettably, we no longer had around us the scenery of a place such as the Xiongyue Hot Springs, but they were growing trees and attempting paddy land work at the hotel, which gave the place a certain rusticity. Because it was so convenient to travel along the trunk line of the railway, the Japanese living in Manchuria frequently came from north and south to enjoy the baths here. It was particularly bustling in the early summer when Russian and Chinese bathers stopped in as well.

We came here and saw a kind of soil that the Chinese call *mianxian* and the Japanese call *sōdachi*: terrain covered with soda. The soil was rich in soda, and it volatilized and turned the surface white as it coagulated. I have heard that there are many such areas throughout Manchuria and Mongolia. Because the region around this hot springs is generally rich in soda, plants and trees do not readily grow, although one variety of acacia does bloom well. My husband wrote a poem here:

Plants, trees, and soil in Tanggangzi all dimly white,
the memory is terribly sad.

About twelve miles to the east of the hot springs lies the famed peak of southern Manchuria known as Qianshan. From the upper floor of the hotel, one face of its sharp, starkly pointed peak can be seen leaning, cutting a gallant figure like Mt. Myōgi, halfway into the sky. We detrained at Tanggangzi Station because we wanted to visit all three of the Manchurian hot springs, but also because we wanted to see the beauty of Qianshan. The writers Ōmachi Keigetsu [1869–1925] and Tayama Katai [1871–1930] had both climbed this mountain, and last autumn the writers Arishima Ikuma [1882–1974] and Masamune Tokusaburō [1883–1962] climbed it as well, led by Mayama Kōji.[5] When they heard that we were going to Manchuria this year, Arishima and Masamune both energetically encouraged us to be sure to go see this mountain. That evening, our guide Mr. Katō spoke with a man at the hotel and took care of preparations for us to climb it the following day. He got Mr. Umehara Shūji, long resident in this area and quite familiar with the mountain, to come along with us.

▬▬

The next morning arrived. Two horses and a sedan chair were waiting in front of the hotel. My husband road one of the horses, and Mr. Katō and Mr. Umehara alternately rode the other horse. The "sedan chair" was a palanquin in the shape of a chair carried by four people, which had been arranged for me. There were two grooms for the horses, four men for the sedan chair, and six coolies carrying blankets and two days' worth of provisions (box lunches, white rice, drinks, sugar, and various canned goods). They were all Chinese, and our party of four set out following a route behind the hotel. My husband's posture—having not ridden a horse in nearly thirty years—seemed rather uncertain over the first few hundred yards, but soon his stirrups and waist seemed to be in good form. Mr. Katō did not look particularly adept at equestrianship either, and when we reached a grassy area he could not keep his horse from craning its neck. My husband didn't see this as he was about to ride ahead of Mr. Katō's horse, but for some reason my husband's horse wouldn't go ahead. We learned from Mr. Umehara's translation that the two horses were used to pulling the same carts, and as second in command Mr. Katō's horse was used to going first while my husband's, being the boss, followed. Thus, even while the horses rode along separately, they maintained their usual order.

Generally speaking, heading north along the trunk line of the South Manchurian Railway, we saw prairie land to the left and numerous mountain peaks to the right. There were fields tucked in between the peaks, rivers stretching out before us, villages dotting the landscape, and glimpses of willow trees among them all. All this made a magnificent view from afar. That day we went toward the fields to our left, and as far as the eye could see was a carpet of soybean and sorghum sprouts barely two inches tall along a long, beautiful ridge in a field. There were thickets of willows here and there, and villages in the distance interspersed among the trees with walls of grayish brown, the same color as the earth. In the bright May sunlight, there was a light wind that day, and the willow catkins, white, flew about in great triumph. When we happened upon a road along which we had to detour, the horses and sedan chair bearers stepped out onto the broad field in a straight line without a moment's thought. This was a practice with which the owner of this field would find no fault, as there were already signs of a shortcut having been made in a straight line where people and horses had traversed the field, as there were on every field. This was farming on an immense scale, and no harm came to the crops because of such a shortcut. One could truly sense that this was something only possible in such a large country.

On this trip I saw for the first time with my own eyes how an insect known as the dung beetle (C. *qianglang*), a kind of gold bug, would ball up bits of oxen and horse manure and transport them to its lair. This is what is described in the phrase of the *Huainanzi:* "The dung beatle plays with balls."[6] When they espy the manure, they pull their wings back and drop to the ground. They push from behind spherical pieces of it about the size of a one-sen copper coin, and roll it across the earth as they move.

▭ ■ ▭

Before long Qianshan was pressing in before us, as we stood on land from which we could see mountains close at hand on both right and left. At a slight distance removed on the left, we could see a bald mountain in reddish brown; it was one of the mines at Anshan where the South Manchurian Railway Company was excavating iron ore. Together with the other mining areas in the region, they calculated the underground deposits to be 200 million tons.

As we approached the southern foothills of Qianshan, there was a small stream known as Nanshan'gou, and facing the stream was a village called Shangshiqiaozi. We opened our lunches at midday in the town inn, asked for some hot water, and drank it with black tea that we had brought along. The Chinese coolies were fed at the inn. Their meal consisted of flour from something like sorghum made into what looked like *mantou* (steamed bread), and they ate by adding fresh leaks to something that added flavor in some sort of broth. The proprietor of the inn politely encouraged us to try these steamed items, but one bite was enough to convince me that for me it was inedible. Their thirst satisfied for the time being, the coolies were happily satiated. When we went to pay, these meals and our tea money came to 50 yuan altogether. Readers may be shocked by our extravagance, but before leaving the hotel I had changed some Japanese money into Fengtian bills. Fifty yuan in Fengtian currency on today's market has fallen to less than two yen. That less than two yen was enough for twelve Chinese coolies to eat their fill, plus provide the four of us with tea money, was a great surprise to me and my husband. This was sufficient for us to conclude just how inexpensive was life for the Chinese in general. They all ate their fill at lunch that day at our expense, and Mr. Umehara said it was a feast for them. Coolies, or physical laborers, from Dalian and elsewhere spend, converted into Japanese currency, between five and ten sen each day on food.

Qianshan belonged to the Changbai branch range, which ran to the southwest from the Sino-Korean border. With its bare granite rocks protruding at every peak some two thousand feet above sea level, it looks like a miniature landscape of a mountain sculpted by the remains of a fierce weathering process, surrounded by forty-eight ravines and rich in precipices and strange rock formations. To soften its rugged, gaunt visage, pine trees, wild pear trees, oak trees, beech trees, and black alders as well as many other varieties dotted the picturesque landscape with the brilliance of the fresh green season. This strange sight of countless peaks, large and small, all confused and mixed together had been called Qiandingshan [lit. "mountain of one thousand peaks"] and Qianhuashan [lit. "mountain of one thousand flowers"], though today it is simple known as Qianshan [lit. "one thousand mountains"]. Occupying scenic spots among the cliffs of the more important peaks, Wusi, Shiguan, Jiugong, and Si'an all convey the architectural grandeur of an earlier era. The Buddhist temples there were mostly built in the Jingde reign period [early eleventh century] of the Song dynasty [960–1279], although those sites today are reconstructions of the Ming and Qing eras. The Daoist shrines were built in the Qianlong period [eighteenth century] of the Qing dynasty, and many were rebuilt thereafter. According to legend, at the time of his invasion of Korea, Emperor Taizong [r. 626–49] of the Tang came through here; it is also said that there are stone tablets dating from the Sui dynasty [589–618]. Contemporary Chinese scholars, however, do not believe these tales.

As best we could, we avoided steep shortcuts and traveled southeast along the foothills from Shangshiqiaozi. We then turned to the left and climbed a mountain along the ravine of the Xiangyan Temple. This ravine was filled with the verdant growth of wild pear trees. Temples and shrines in the mountains provide homes for many Buddhist monks and Daoist priests, and one resource for a comparatively comfortable life is the great quantity of firewood from all the mountains, though I have heard that the fruit from the pear trees provides another source of food.

The Xiangyan Temple backed on to a precipice that looked like a screen where the ravine came to a dead end, and there was a meditation hall and a guest hall outside the Hall of the Buddha. Surrounded by mountains, there was no wide vista to look out onto, but it was quiet just listening to the sounds of the wind blowing through the pines above the rocks. At a nearby peak, the Jinli Pagoda of the famous Yuan-era monk Xue'an could be seen with the pale blue appearance of antiquity about it. The guest hall, as the name indicates, was a meditational cell to welcome guests who had come on pilgrimage. These were always attached to Chinese temples. There was a hearth for boiling tea water in the center, and table and chairs were arranged and a *kang* [a brick bed warmed by fire] set up in the left and the right rooms. On one side was the priests' quarters and on the other the guest room. We relaxed in the guest hall, drinking tea poured for us by a young child. When we finished drinking, the child refilled our cups several times, as was the custom when receiving guests, not only in temples but in China generally. The monks just exchanged a few words, not saying a great deal, as befit the situation.

———■■■———

As soon as we left the Xiangyan Temple, turned left off the central path of the ravine, and came out onto a level road in the mountains, we saw up on the left side the Platform of the Immortals, the highest peak among those comprising Qianshan. After gradually proceeding about 2.5 miles to the north, we again turned to the left and entered another ravine. We were not moving straight up a precipitous peak, so I got down from the sedan chair and walked. The men had earlier returned the horses at Shangshiqiaozi, so we were all now walking. When we came to a fork in the road, Mr. Umehara, who had acquired experience as a guide, lost his way for a moment because the landmark grove of trees had been cut down, but when we climbed to the top of this sharp cliff, the many peaks within the Qianshan complex became visible, and just then, in the evening light, everyone instinctively called out, "What beautiful scenery!" We then descended a bit, and there was a road going up the peak to the left. We had not come across it before, and it went among the strange rock formations and pine trees, leading to our objective, the Da'an Temple.

Before the front gate of the Da'an Temple, a tall wild pear tree had sprouted flowers that looked like those of a white peach tree. The seasons came later here than in the valley of the Xiangyan Temple. When we entered, stepping over high stone steps, purple clouds, penetrating the light of nightfall, gathered over the garden in front of the main sanctuary, and we were struck by a beautiful fragrance. Lilacs—what the Chinese call *ʐidingxiang*—had been planted in this yard and were now in full bloom. The evening Buddhist religious service had just begun. The door of the main sanctuary was open, the sound of bells rang in the mountains, and the temple monks—over ten in all—emerged from their quarters and entered the main sanctuary. All were attired in the dark gray robes of Buddhist priests, though without the Buddhist stole. We forgot the weariness of our feet and, following the priests from behind, stood before the sanctuary. The main image was of the Buddha. Here in this temple the priests maintained their dignity well, as they lit the candles, burnt incense, and several times knelt and worshipped. One priest sounded the priests' bell in unison while reading from the sutras. Amid all this, the scene of frequent kneeling in prayer was one of utter solemnity. Compared to the formulaic manner in which young priests in Japan utter Buddhist scripture, one felt that the older style of devotion remained alive here. As for musical instruments, in addition to the bell, they also sounded the priestly gong.

The Da'an Temple is said to be the oldest among the five great temples of Qianshan. On the grounds there are, in addition to the Hall of the Buddha, a Vedas pavilion, and its recently touched up red and green coloring was magnificent. There was as well a spacious priests' quarters, a kitchen, and guest rooms that had recently undergone repairs, and aside from the restrooms all were relatively clean. There were no main pillars in Manchurian homes, and the level structure of the roofs are frequently referred to as *pingfang* in the *Wei shu* (History of the Northern Wei Dynasty).[7] These Buddhist and Daoist temples in the mountains seem to have preserved the old style of tile roofing on a heightened roof. Like individual homes in the area, the walls of temples are made of solid gray-black bricks; we did not see a single one made of packed earth, as is the Japanese style. This temple was constructed with its back to a peak known as Mount Baotai, and the peaks on the other three sides accentuated the beauty, with cliffs and wonderful rock formations. Pine and other trees scattered among them create a fine scene of nature. To the south the view is open, and the mountains within Qianshan can be seen in all their splendor. Thus, in his *Qianshan youji* (Travelogue of Qianshan), Zhang Wenzhen of the Qing period wrote, "I daresay that of the temples of Qianshan Da'an is the most picturesque." It was regrettable, though, that for a place so relatively rich in ravines, the beauty of the waterways of Qianshan was rather poor. Furthermore, their drinking water was drawn from a well among the rocks below, but for us Japanese, with our fastidiousness, we were thoroughly hampered by being unable to use the water even to wash our hands.

The four of us stayed overnight in the guest quarters, while the Chinese coolies slept in the kitchen. They cooked the rice they had carried for us and added it to the canned goods and pickles with which the hotel had provided us, and we partook of dinner by a dimly lit three-wicked lamp. With the sound of steam gallantly reverberating in a brass samovar, a temple boy boiled hot water and poured us tea; he liked the food we had left over and carried it off with him. It was the mountain temple custom when evening arrived for all to go to sleep early, without lighting candles. As our lamp was low, we were rather disinclined to chat. And so we had no choice but to go to sleep at 8:00 P.M. with Chinese bedding over a kang the size of three tatami mats. The bedbugs we had feared in the recently repaired guest quarters never materialized, and the bedding had just been washed, which, contrary to our expectations, was very pleasant. It was still quite cold at night, and the young boy had earlier lit the kang from outside. We were soon soundly asleep from this warmth and our daytime exhaustion. In the middle of the night, though, I was suddenly awakened, as the mountain wind from the rocks and the pine trees blew thunderously through the window. I had never stayed at the peak of such gaunt, deserted, old rocky mountains, and I felt something rising in my mind awakened from slumber upon which I quietly reflected. It was not the familiarity of nature but the belovedness of humanity. One after the next I pondered our children back in Tokyo, my friends, and people I had only just met in Dalian. My husband who had similarly awakened was mindful of the smell of the lamp filling the room with smoke, and he got up, opened the door, and for a time went outside. He returned saying, "The sky is magnificently full of stars!" He wrote in his diary as follows:

Waking in the wee hours of the night, I softly pushed open the door and stepped outside. The deep blue sky was filled with stars as crystal clear as in autumn. A zephyr played the quiet musical sounds through the pine trees of the cliffs, a vision of sublime beauty far, far from humanity. I have not seen Mount Tai in Shandong, but I have heard from others who visited it that it has become vulgarized. The vast otherworldly elegance that can be glimpsed in the mountain-climbing poems of Li Bo [701–62] seems rather now to reside here in Qianshan.

The monks of Da'an Temple had begun their morning prayers by 4:00 the following morning, and the sound of bells awakened us in the dim light of the guests' quarters. A sweet sensation beyond this realm of dust hearkened us to the Buddhist phrases at daybreak. The mountain water the boy at the temple ladled out was clear and cold as ice. We measured out small amounts to wash our faces, and the coolies who accompanied us then prepared breakfast for us. Mr. Umehara said that they were extraordinarily frugal with the water drawn from the deep ravines. The priests washed their faces with a single pan of it. First, the head priest washed his face, and then in order the other priests did likewise with the same water until finally it became so dirty one could not see the bottom of the pan. Furthermore, it seemed that the priests had become inured to and no longer paid heed to uncleanliness.

While we were eating breakfast, the steward priest fried in oil a fresh blossom from a tree whose name escapes me and said we should eat it as a side dish. It was thickly coated with oil, and everyone took just a small taste. I laughed and said, "The food of hermits does not suit our palate."

My husband opened a book sitting on the table in the guest quarters and found that it was the *Jin'gang jing rushuo zhu* (Annotated Commentary on the Diamond Sutra), published in Daoguang 26 [1846] of the Qing dynasty. Although not an ancient edition, the style of the commentary was extraordinary, and my husband told the steward priest that he would like to purchase it. The priest could not sell it, but said that if he so wished he would give my husband the work as a present, and so my husband was only too happy to accept it. Also on the table was a book published just the year before last, a small text entitled the *You Qianshan ji* (Account of Travels in Qianshan) by Chen Xingya. The priest gave this book to my husband as well. As compensation for these, my husband donated a piece of gold to the temple. The priest told us that the temple held many Ming- and Qing-era texts as well as a few Song editions, but we did not have the time to ask to see them. Inasmuch as none of the mountain temples charged room-and-board fees, as we were about to leave, following Mr. Umehara's instruction, we left 100 yuan in Fengtian currency as compensation for the ten of us in the group. This amounts to less than four Japanese yen. We climbed Mount Baotai behind Da'an Temple for a while and turned to the right, where we came upon the spectacular scenery of the Arhat Grottos. There, of course, are enshrined eight rough, modern, colored arhat images in the caves about eighteen feet deep. The cave reaches an impasse and there, as a window of nature, it opens midway onto the overhanging cliffs and looks out before one's feet onto the sky to the east of Qianshan and the acme of various peaks. The magnificance of the view comes from the sense that one has here a many-storeyed building in the sky. The wind blowing in from the stone window was bracingly chilly and thus would not permit one to linger with the view. We all regretted not having climbed in warmer weather.

We headed from there to the northwest, descending along a steep defile into a grove of trees. After climbing tall stone steps at Mount Jingping, we paid a visit to the Zhonghui Temple. We paid our respects at the Hall of Prosperity (with its Buddha of the Ten Deeds, Guanyin or Goddess of Mercy, and God of the Earth) and the Ciyun Pavilion (with its Sakyamuni, Amitabha, and God of Medicine), and then rested for a short time in the guest quarters with some tea. The beauty of the temple structures remained from repairs made in the Qing era, but it was a bit more run down than Da'an Temple. It was also inferior in its elegance. The floor of the Hall of the Buddha was on a different level from the guest quarters, and, interestingly, water could be drawn from one well there at either level. It was dubbed *lianhua shuangjing* (dual lotus wells) and was counted as one of the sixteen scenic sites of this temple.

From there we entered a valley to the north and descended in a southerly direction. We climbed a mountain that took us as far as Wujing Monastery, one of the ten Daoist monasteries of Qianshan. It was only slightly less magnificent than Da'an Temple and is an outstanding example of the Daoist temples in Manchuria. The grounds form the shape of a rocky human belly, divided into left and right. At the main sanctuary to the right, people pray to the three emperors of heaven, earth, and water; to the left, the Daoist priests' quarters and guest rooms are located. There was also a Guanyin Hall, indicating that contemporary Daoism had intermixed with Buddhism. However, this space had once housed the Zuyue Temple, and in the late Ming or early Qing dynasty a Daoist priest by the name of Liu Tailin had inaugurated a Daoist monastery on these grounds.

After we first paid our respects at the main sanctuary, we circled around to the stone steps leading up a peak behind it until we reached the top. This spot was a steep declivity known popularly as *xianren biansuo* (the hermits' toilet). From it one could look out onto the ravines and peaks of Qianshan. In one direction, an immense rock known as the "stone of heaven's platform" caught our attention. When we reached its summit, we discovered the most extraordinary of views. Another view from this rock looked out onto a precipice some four or five feet below, and at a creep we intruded on this inaccessible spot, since we had to scale it. Mr. Chen, author of *You Qianshan ji,* who wrote his work here, had built a thin metal railing as a convenience to future climbers who ascended to take in the view. However, the metal rod inserted into the rock had become rickety, and I thus declined to climb further. My husband returned after ascending halfway. Mr. Katō and Mr. Umehara had both already made this climb. A Daoist priest lived in a hut in these environs.

We retraced our steps and returned to the guest quarters, where there were now many Daoist priests. They were all wearing clear blue garments and quietly greeted us. All were men of a superior, unworldly cast of mind, which reminded me of a painting of Daoists and Buddhists mingling together. Unlike Buddhist monks, they had all grown thin beards. One among them was a man just thirty years of age, innocent, slender, and tall, with a fair complexion and bright eyes. This priest reminded me of Akutagawa Ryūnosuke [1892–1927] in appearance.[8] All the priests had a composed demeanor, and, while wearing faint smiles on their faces, chatted about something or other in low voices. They seemed a different race of men from the contemporary Chinese we ordinarily think of. Perhaps there were among them Daoist priests of a more corrupt nature, but on the surface none of them would even approach a woman, and like the monks at Da'an Temple they would not eat meat, preferring a life of abstinence. Those who wish to see genuine Daoist priests in Manchuria would be well advised to climb Qianshan. On the table in the guest quarters was a pile of modern Shanghai editions of various ancient Chinese texts. We had not imagined that looking out over the mountain peaks from a window thrown open amid the rocks, listening to the wind in the pine trees, and sipping tea poured for us by a young boy while quietly and agreeably sitting across from these Daoist priests were things of the modern era. The flowers buds on a lone red peach tree still blooming beside a nearby stone wall reminded me of the enchanted land one encountered in old Chinese texts. Here we stopped to eat the lunches that the coolies had prepared for us at Da'an Temple, but cutting up smelly, canned ham was hardly appropriate to the situation, and my conscience reproached me with respect to the Daoist priests.

Zuyue Temple is just as old as Da'an Temple, but it is now in a state of decay, and only the main sanctuary remains in existence. From the cliffs of the Wujing Monastery we did no more than peer down at it.

We left the Wujing Monastery and headed down into the valley, then further on turned right, climbed a hill, and came to Longquan Temple. We had heard that of the five temples of Qianshan only the monks here lived a more secular life. Before treading on the stone steps and entering the tower gate, a monk standing above us asked Mr. Umehara how the market that day had been for Fengtian currency. Longquan Temple was built in the fifth year of the reign of the Longqing Emperor, Muzong, of the Ming dynasty (1566) and had been repaired on several occasions later during the Qing dynasty. It was constructed on an immense scale in the mountains, with the structure of its halls and pavilions exceeding those of Da'an Temple. However, because of the lowness of the mountains and the decadence of the resident monks, a sense of quiet refinement was difficult to come by here. The numerous extraordinary rock formations inside and outside the temple were no different from the other temples and monasteries, but nowhere else had we been, for example, encouraged to buy a souvenir walking stick. Disinclined to spend a night here, we changed our plans and decided to return that very day to Tanggangzi. Reluctantly we passed up a climb the following day of Wufo Summit, one of the famed scenic spots of Qianshan.

At a hillock that headed south into the ravine at Longquan Temple, we came upon several woodcutters who were running down the steap incline as nimbly as monkeys, having felled a grove of trees from the peak and burdened with the long trunks of the trees. This was rough work the likes of which Japanese woodsmen were incapable of doing. The sound when the tree trunks hit the rocks at the lower end of the grove shook the mountain with a roar. We then turned and headed west, climbed another mountain, and looked up to the Pu'an Monastery and Wufo Summit on a peak to our right. The mountain had a gradual descent, and we proceeded along a path that made a sharp turn at Shangshiqiaozi from yesterday. There was a home there where a donkey with blinders was walking around a stone mill, making flour from sorghum. Perhaps in the donkey's mind, he was pulling a heavy object ahead along a long road, but he was in fact going in circles around the same spot over and over. The sound of the millstone reverberated monotonously in this hut in the forest, giving the feel of the mountains an even greater sense of loneliness. I was reflecting on the fact that although mankind is numerous, we live out our lives in circumstances not terribly different from this donkey, and I sympathized with the animal's irredeemable fate.

When we had finished climbing down Qianshan, we passed in front of the inn where we had spent the night in Shangshiqiaozi and then took the road to the north. We proceeded to Taigushan, one of the iron ore regions of Anshan, and from there caught a ride on a train on the narrow-gauge railway that moved ore from Anshan until we arrived at the Anshan Station on the trunk line of the South Manchurian Railway. Ancient graves from the Han dynasty [206 B.C.E.–220 C.E.], the Koguryŏ era [37 B.C.E.–668 C.E.], and the Liao [907–1125] and Jin [1115–1234] periods are scattered here and could be spotted throughout this area. Mr. Katō pointed out to us in the field between Shangshiqiaozi and Xiashiqiaozi the remains of ancient graves that just a few years ago Professor Torii Ryūzō [1870–1953] had excavated.⁹ Torii was touring Manchuria and Mongolia at the same time as we were, and we later learned that, about a month after we visited this area, he had discovered Nestorian (ancient Christian) crosses from a successful dig in the tombs in this area.

Mr. Katō looked at his watch. Only forty more minutes until the last train, a little past 5:00 P.M., left Taigushan. He then sent one of the Chinese porters ahead to make sure that the train would depart late. The other sedan chair bearers and coolies said, "If we send you off to Taigushan, then walk along the road for fifteen or sixteen miles, we won't make it back to Tanggangzi this evening. If we stay over night, we'll have to pay for lodging, so why don't we all take the train back together?" When Umehara and Katō agreed, the coolies suddenly began moving much more rapidly. The sedan chair carrying me, in particular, raced along as if it had wings and arrived first at Taigushan Station, having covered over five miles from Shangshiqiaozi in only forty minutes. My husband and Messrs. Katō and Umehara also kept this forced march pace and arrived a few minutes later. I was stunned at the extraordinary capacities of Chinese laborers who only ate a small amount of principally steamed bread made from wheat flour usually together with vegetables—and fish or meat only a few times each year. In Dalian the wharf coolies hauled immense weights of six or seven tons on average each day, and I witnessed laborers amid the intense heat of oil and glass factories. I experienced this again with the sedan chair bearers who carried me. Mr. Fujiyama Kazuo of the Fukushō kakō Company in Dalian, which was indirectly managed by the South Manchurian Railway Company, gave me a recently published work based on detailed experiences with Chinese laborers entitled *Saishoku to rōdō mondai* (Vegetarian Diet and the Labor Issues).

When the narrow-gauge rail line carrying us arrived at An-shan Station, it was already dusk, not a good time to see the South Manchurian Railway's iron works. Soon a train on the trunk line arrived from the north, and we boarded it to return to the Tanggangzi Hot Springs. After bathing, we had dinner with Katō and Umehara. We spoke of the stunning scenery and steep pathways of Qianshan and thanked them for guiding us through it. We were encouraged to climb Qianshan again during the season of autumnal foliage.

After noon the following day, Mr. Nishida Inosuke arrived in Tanggangzi from Dalian. As we had planned, he had come this long distance to spend his Sunday with us reciting poetry. Mr. Katō soon joined us and we convened our meeting of tanka poets. We began before dinner, then read something aloud, and again late in the evening read a second piece of work. Although Mr. Nishida had been a writer for twenty years, Mr. Katō, who was also a poet, began reciting his poems from that day with special enthusiasm, perhaps because his senses had been so aroused by Qianshan. Actually, though, it wasn't from that day, for already the previous day when we were still in the mountains Katō had several times given us examples of poetry.

That evening the poet Satō Sōnosuke also arrived. He had left Tokyo after us, and we had bumped into him in Dalian and Jinzhou. We were overjoyed that from tomorrow on this young, cheerful poet would be joining our party. We boarded a train the following morning for Liaoyang, while Mr. Nishida planned to return to Dalian somewhat later.

LIAOYANG

The oldest city still extant in Manchuria is Liaoyang in the province of Fengtian. The author of the text *Liaodong wenxian zhenglüe*, noted earlier, had shown by textual exegesis that the "Xiangping cheng" mentioned in the "Geographical Treatise" of the *Han shu* (History of the Han Dynasty) was the present-day city of Liaoyang. In the terrain to the east of the city, the Guangyou Temple had been built during the Eastern (or Former) Han dynasty, and a pagoda 230 feet high, in the shape of an octagon, with thirteen storeys of white marble tiles, had stood on the temple grounds since the Koguryŏ era. The temple hall stood until modern times when it was destroyed by Russians who were laying track for the Chinese Eastern Railway. Only the pagoda now remained, the famed White Pagoda of Liaoyang. Because we had been primarily interested in seeing this pagoda, we detrained at the Liaoyang Station on the trunk line of the South Manchurian Railway. It was about two-thirds of a mile from the station to the city, and this terrain all now belonged to the South Manchurian Railway, which also managed the Japanese city within Liaoyang. There was a central boulevard some 24 yards wide lined with beautiful elm trees that extended in a straight line from the station. The remains of the Guangyou Temple also belonged to land under the control of the South Manchurian Railway Company and were only about 100 yards from the station. On the left side of the central boulevard was a White Pagoda Park built by Japanese. The White Pagoda looked out onto a plain that began several miles before reaching the station. Leaving the public square before the station, its faint white, elegant, round image greeted us with a smile from the willow treetops in the park.

We had sent our luggage ahead to the hotel in Liaoyang, and then with some people who had come to meet us we promptly entered this park and walked to the base of the White Pagoda. Buddhist images were inset in the concave depressions on the four sides shaped as octagons, and Buddhist images looked out in relief from each of the convex portions of the four walls. Lacking the requisite connoisseurship in such matters, I could make no meaningful judgments, but everyone said they closely resembled the appearance of Buddhas from China's Six Dynasties period [220–589] and the relief images were remarkable. Although the pagoda itself seemed to have been repaired a number of times, exposed as it had been for so long to the wind and rain, it was in a serious state of dilapidation. Particularly in the upper storey there were hundreds of birds flying around a large group of stone swallows nesting. With the wind blowing through willow catkins, which flew about as in a dream beneath the warm blue sky of early summer, I felt a certain happiness tinged with a faint pathos as I looked up at the ancient declining pagoda. But when I turned my gaze, the sight close by of Japanese and Western buildings in the Japanese city struck a sharply discordant note.

In the park were the Liaoyang Shinto Shrine and the South Manchurian Railway Club, both built by Japanese. Only a few days earlier, the lower floor of the club had been used as billetting for infantrymen dispatched unexpectedly from Korea. We ate on the upper floor, and I was welcomed with a luncheon banquet by the wives of the Women's Association of Japanese resident there. The South Manchurian Railway Company had established a Society Bureau at various sites that planned for the well-being of company employees and their families away from home. Here Mr. Sugimoto Shunki, director of the Society Bureau, was in charge of the affairs of the women's association and the youth group. Mr. Sugimoto was a Christian who had worked for a social welfare agency when he lived in Yokohama. After lunch I had a photo taken together with the women and then headed for the Liaodong Hotel. It was called a "hotel" but was actually a Japanese style *ryokan*, or inn, that faced out onto the central boulevard. The White Pagoda stood behind the building nearby. Because of the troops from Korea lodged there, we were unable to enter the rooms on the lower floor from which we could have seen the park. The officers and soldiers who came and went appeared in an excited state, as though a war was commencing. Imperialism and the smell of liquor rippled through, and the atmosphere of this inn became thoroughly incompatible with our desire to write poems about the gentle White Pagoda and the willow catkins. We entered a poorly lit room in a corner of the lower floor, and for a time could not even bring ourselves to open our bags and change clothes.

At two o'clock in the afternoon, we divided into two carriages and went on a tour of the city. We were particularly fortunate to have Mr. Wakabayashi Hyōkichi, principal of the Commercial School and a scholar of the Chinese language, serve as our guide. The city of Liaoyang has a consecutive history spanning two thousand years during which it has undergone many changes. After the Manchu defeat of the armies of the Ming dynasty here in the third lunar month of 1621 (Tianming 6), Liaoyang served as the Qing capital until Emperor Taizu [Nurhaci] moved his capital to Shenyang (present-day Fengtian).[10] It is surrounded by a wall that runs some 2.5 miles east to west and about 1.6 miles north to south, with six gates leading into and out of the city. It is located at the confluence of the Hun River (formerly known as the Xiaoliang River) and the Taizu River (formerly known as the Daliang River), since antiquity said to be a fortress site. The center of the city has a main intersection and four boulevards spreading out to the north, south, east, and west; there are, in addition, numerous smaller roads.

This was the way that from olden days Chinese cities were laid out. The most bustling areas of the city were the great markets at the eastern and western gates, and, as was the case in other cities, opulent mansions belonging to men of stature were scattered along the back streets.

According to Mr. Wakabayashi, that was the extent of the old city, for scarcely anything of importance remained of the ancient architecture worth seeing. Everything was in ruins. He then said he would take us to an extraordinary site, and we proceeded to visit a Chinese court and prison. He had made the arrangements in advance, and we were expected by Mr. Liu Bingzao, the chief public prosecutor. He showed us the courtroom, the defendants' waiting room, and the lawyers' waiting room, offering explanations along the way. It all seemed to be based on the Japanese court system, the scale resembling a local court in Japan. The fixtures were simple, neater than I had imagined. At the prison the warden, Mr. Shi Yuheng, showed us around his institution. The cells, too, were cleaner than expected, indeed cleaner than ordinary Chinese homes. In the middle of each cell was a raised bed on a kang floor heater over which straw matting was laid out. In each cell there were either five or seven prisoners seated politely in the lotus position. In the winter, the kang was lit from behind the wall. I admired the fact that you would find this only in the prisons of a cold country. I wonder if even in Japan the prisons of Hokkaidō are outfitted with heaters. I also admired the orderly rules under which each of the prisoners had his bedding neatly folded and stacked behind them. Above the cell door was a wire screen through which one could see inside, and above the screen the prisoner's surname and crime was posted. Women's prison cells were equally well ordered. The young poet Mr. Satō Sōnosuke, who was with our party, noticed that there was a beautiful woman among the women prisoners, but he was even more stunned to read that her crime was murder. I had the sense that, on the whole, the prisoners—men and women both—seemed in better physical shape than the laborers we had seen in private homes; perhaps their standard light blue prison uniforms afforded them this air.

———■———

Mr. Wakabayashi also took us to see an opium den. It was located along a narrow alley crowded with brothels and eateries. The brothel next door was a small house with one door and a single room. The sight of a prostitute (between fourteen and twenty years of age) standing in the door, beckoning to potential customers was too painful to watch. Above the door into the opium den hung a sign reading, "Restricted Opium Use Here." By moderating and eventually bringing an end to opium smoking, the authorities actually allowed opium use, which they then taxed as a source of revenue for the Fengtian government. In recent years, Zhang Zuolin [1875–1928] had been compelling farmers in the Northeast to cultivate opium for the same reason that he could extract a heavy tax on it.[11] This opium den was a run-down house, not the sort of place frequented by persons of wealth. In the center of the room was an earthen floor, and several customers were lying prostrate on their sides on bed matting to the left and right as they smoked opium. People were wearing whatever they happened to have on. Already completely intoxicated, they were adrift in the land of dreams, sleeping with their faces turned upward. With the flame from a hand-held lantern, an assistant enabled those customers half-awake and half in a daze to smoke from the large pipe bowl full of opium the color of refined dark sugar. Not a single customer there seemed to notice us looking at them. Perhaps they were lost at the peak of their pleasurable dreams, but to those of us looking on it was a wretched, horrific sight.

Mr. Wakabayashi also escorted us to the temple of the city god (*chenghuang miao*) at Jinyin'gang. As readers of *Liaozhai zhi yi* (Strange Stories from a Chinese Studio) know, a *chenghuang miao* is a temple at which one prays to the guardian deity for the city. The deity was not fixed, but it had become the custom that they prayed to local persons of renown or wisdom from the past who had worked for the public interest. The temple had been a mixture of Daoism and Buddhism, much like the Shinto-Buddhist amalgam common in Japan, and it seemed as well that all manner of superstitious observances were performed here. We had seen this already at the Tianqi Shrine in Jinzhou, but there was also a stove set up in front of this temple at which on festival days they burned paper money.

We also visited Buddhist temples and a Lamaist pagoda in Liaoyang, and, as an example of the home of a wealthy official, Professor Wakabayashi showed us the mansion of Yu Chonghan [1871–1932], the former commission of commerce of Fengtian. After the sightseeing was over, we headed for a dinner party at the South Manchurian Railway Club, sponsored by a group of Japanese volunteeers living abroad. Seated there, I met Mibōta Tsuruo, office manager for the South Manchurian Railway Company, Sukegawa Tokuhai, the police chief, and ten or more others. Afterward, my husband, Mr. Satō, and I gave lectures in a large room on the upper floor of the club. Over two hundred local Japanese attended.

Our rooms in the hotel faced onto a major thoroughfare, and the next morning we were awakened at 3:00 A.M. when, at that early hour, the horses and vehicles of Chinese laborers passed by. We went to the station where the people we had met the previous day sent us off. Mr. Nakamura Shin of the Electric Light Company brought several specimens of old coins recently unearthed from ancient graves in the area, and Professor Wakabayashi brought a valuable book presented by the Qianlong Emperor to a Manchu bannerman by the name of Fu-hui in the thirty-third year of his reign (1768). We were overjoyed to receive both as presents. Director Sugimoto went out of his way and rode with us as far as the next station at Zhangtaizi, and during the ride he recounted to us his impressions of life for Japanese living in Manchuria. One point he made, about the difficulty faced by Japanese women born and raised in Manchuria in finding husbands, struck me as particularly melancholy.

ON BOARD THE AN-FENG LINE

At Sujiatun Station on the trunk line of the South Manchurian Railway, we changed to the An-Feng line heading toward Andong. Having been moving in a northerly direction, we now switched our itinerary to the east. This rail line was rich in mountain and river landscapes; it was lush with trees, and suddenly we felt as though we were traveling within Japan. En route there was a city at Lake Benxi at the confluence of the Huoliansai River and the Taizi River. This place was famous for the coal mines and iron ore of the Caitie Company jointly managed by the Ōkura Corporation and the Chinese. They say that there are some 200 million tons of semi-anthracite coal buried there and 80 million tons altogether of magnetite. In addition, there is the Niuxintai coal mine, a Sino-Japanese joint venture. After leaving Qiaotou Station, the train entered a ravine of the Xi River, and the immense bedrock above the blue expanse of water made a formidable sight. There stood the Puji Temple. They called this bedrock "angler's platform"; when we came upon it suddenly, deep in the secluded mountains, it appeared as if in a dream. I left the train at Qiaotou Station, regretting that I had no time to spend sightseeing in this area. Although I could only see it from one side of the train, I thoroughly enjoyed the fresh verdure of the season. It would surely be even more enjoyable to stand on a one-hundred-foot precipice and walk around, taking in the complete effect when everything was in full bloom.

Fenghuangcheng is the only city on the An-Feng line that lies in a basin. Its prosperity is said to rival that of Andong in recent years. Unfortunately, we had not made plans to get off the train at this station. About five miles southeast of the city the famed Fenghuang mountains formed at their peaks a sharp wall of mysterious crags that resembled Qianshan. We were told that scattered in the ravines of the mountains were a number of ancient temples and Buddhist and Daoist houses of prayer, that there were as well the remains of cities dating to the Koguryŏ period, and that the area was rich in scenery as the mountains hugged the rail line. Fortunately, all the way to the next stop, at Sansi Station, the imposing presence of the mountains came into our range of vision through the train window and made us feel comfortable.

ANDONG

We arrived in Andong before 5:00 P.M. Passengers coming and going on the train to Korea had to undergo inspection by the Japanese customs officials at the station. It was here that we saw a detestable sight. A group of second- or third-year middle school students on their way back to Japan after sightseeing in Manchuria were about to board a train from Andong through Korea. While under the guidance of their teacher, they laid out their few personal effects suitable for young pupils by the two pillars under the poorly lit railroad overpass at the station, awaiting inspection by the customs officials. We detrained and walked by in front of them, and noticed that on top of the personal items the youngsters had placed on the ground were from two to as many as five or six packets of foreign or Chinese cigarettes, ten to a pack, purchased in Manchuria. There was no reason whatsoever to assume that Japanese youths who were forbidden from smoking at home had bought them for their own use. Clearly, they had bought these cheap cigarettes, not subject to heavy taxes, as token gifts for their fathers and elder brothers back home. It seemed as well that the teacher had bought more cigarettes than allowed and was distributing them among the students to carry back for him. Whatever the case may have been, I felt great pity for these students who had not yet reached the smoking age at the sight of the cigarettes lined up on top of their personal things and quickly looked askance as we passed by. If these were cigarettes purchased as pitiful souvenirs for fathers and brothers, then how pathetic it was to make them open their bags to public view, like the hand luggage of crafty merchants, and inspect them coldheartedly. If these were cigarettes distributed by the teacher for the students to carry back for him, then it was highly imprudent of the teacher to make these underage youngsters do such a thing. Yet, even if this teacher was a university professor whose ordinary salary was extremely low, these people would never have engaged in one-thousandth of the malicious and outrageous acts performed by militarists, politicians, and big financiers. Had such people returned from an occasional trip abroad with three hundred or five hundred cheap cigarettes, in my own sense of ethics I would not feel this to be something bad. To allow teachers who are ordinarily so poor and hardworking such a level of material enjoyment is not something to find fault with. This is not something the state is taking much of a loss on. Because the avenue for tolerance to this extent is not open to the state, teachers must, it appears, resort to using their pupils to carry cigarettes for them. I was exceedingly sympathetic at this unpleasant scene in which the law did not take into consideration human feelings and a sense of humanity.

We were met at the station by South Manchurian Railway Company people as well as by lumber company people and their wives. The wife of Mr. Ōta Hidejirō, former director of the Andong Stock Exchange, also came by herself. The wife of the Japanese consul, Mr. Okada Ken'ichi, sent a car to meet us. We promptly entered it and learned that preparations had been made on our behalf to stay in the consulate that night. However, we had made reservations at the Andong Hotel in front of the station in advance. Thus, while greatly appreciative of Mrs. Okada's kindnesses, we declined and together with Messrs. Satō and Katō checked into the hotel. Soon thereafter we responded to an invitation to dinner at the consulate.

The city of Andong sits on a plain sixteen miles from a large estuary on the western shore of the Yalu River; unfolding from the northwest to the southeast, it spans the Sha River, which comes from the west and enters the Yalu. It is divided into the northeast, known as the old city—namely, the Chinese city—and the southwest, known as the new city—the Japanese city. The Chinese city began significantly to thrive after the Russo-Japanese War, and until then it was a village known as Shahezhen. The Japanese city survived the Russo-Japanese War intact and was rebuilt because it served as a link between the Korean and Manchurian railways. On the opposite shore lies Korea, a large railroad bridge linking the Korean city of Sinŭiju with Andong. West of Andong lies two mountains, Zhenjiang and Yuanbao, and on the mountainside of Yuanbao sit the Andong Shinto Shrine and the Japanese consulate. At the consulate dinner we met a number of people including Mr. and Mrs. Okada, Mr. and Mrs. Naitō Taisuke of the lumber company, Mrs. Yoshida, and Mr. Awano Shun'ichi, who was head of the local office of the South Manchurian Railway Company. The consul and his wife were jovial people full of interest in art and literature, and Mrs. Naitō was a close personal friend of my friend, Adachi Nagako, from their days at Tokyo Women's Senior Normal School. Furthermore, Mrs. Yoshida had been a student at Atomi Women's School over thirty years earlier when my husband taught there. For me it was a thoroughly enjoyable, candid dinner party that I hadn't thought possible for a first meeting. Resplendently beautiful, rose-colored flowers arranged in a vase on the table aroused me from travel weariness. That I learned from the young and gracious Mrs. Okada that the flowers were known in Chinese as *huamancao* made this flower a happy memory for me. After dinner, Consul Okada escorted us to the outside balcony on the roof where lanterns had already been lit. He pointed out and explained to us the city of Andong by night from our bird's-eye view. We then proceeded to the South Manchurian Railway Club and took part in prearranged speeches that began at 8:00 P.M.

Owing to the kindness of the lumber company, we were able to board a steam launch the next morning and set out from the wharf in the Japanese city. We traveled some five miles up the Yalu River, went to a spot from whence we could see Jiulianisheng in the mountains to the left and Tongjunting in the mountains on the Korean side to the right and then returned. Although the river has been called the Yalu in documents since antiquity, local Chinese refer to it as the Dajiang (Great River). This is comparable to our calling the Sumida River the Ōkawa (Great River). It begins in the western foothills of the distant Baitou Mountains, midway comes into the Xuchuan River and Changjin River, and nearer runs into the Hun River and the Ai River. Altogether about 350 miles in length, this river, with its low volume of water, has a river bed with steep slopes and numerous reefs. Steamships with greater than four-foot drafts find it difficult to navigate from the mouth of the river to Andong. Although the amount of water increases after a rain these days, the steam launch continually surveys the water depth as it moves upstream, and this depth will not exceed two feet. Junks ply these waters as far as one hundred miles up, trading in commodities along the upper reaches of the river, and the quantity of upriver trade seems to be increasing each year. Principal among the items involved is the timber, which is taken by raft from the great timber region upstream.

The nearby area had originally been one with a wide river; a number of land masses large and small had long ago emerged in it and formed islands from which had sprung up willow trees and rushes, all changing the landscape of the river. It was still too early for the high season of floating rafts, though we were able to spot a few of them here and there. In the form of junks, in that they raised a sail and flew a crimson flag above the mast, these rafts enveloped the clouds at the peaks on the river, each one rising far and near above the next. Reflecting the green of reeds and willows, they glistened brightly, and as they leisurely sailed down the river they evoked the happy appearance of ridding themselves of modern machine civilization. From time to time, tattered clouds came and went and a light rain fell; the consul, his wife, Mrs. Naitō, and Mrs. Yoshida—all of whom were accompanying us—crouched down in the narrow ship's cabin. From its window we could see the India-ink landscape of nature as the river upstream and the peaks on both shores changed shapes in the clouds. The evening rain on the Xiao River of southern China, which appears in a Chinese poem, seemed to me like what I heard on ship. The Chinese poem from the Tang period floated into my mind, awakened on deck after the rain stopped:

> Resting my chin on my hands, I looked one thousand
> *li*,
> The smoky scene taking more than one shape,
> The distant peaks all different sizes,
> A single mast amid the wind and water.

The steam launch went further downstream from the wharf from whence we initially departed. We passed a large steel bridge, saw the storehouse of the lumber company, and then returned to the wharf. After eating lunch at the hotel, we did some writing that had been requested of us, and then I waited for my husband to return from a visit to his old friend, Mr. Ōta, who was ill. Led by Mr. Yamamoto Ken'ichi, director of the local Society Bureau of the South Manchurian Railway Company, we did some sightseeing by car of the new and old cities, and we also went separately to pay visits to the consulate and the business office of the South Manchurian Railway Company. Our time was limited, though, and we had no choice but to reluctantly pass up crossing the large steel bridge and treading on Korean soil on the other side. At 4:00 P.M. we again boarded a train on the An-Feng line, as our plans called for us to travel back to the third station from there, Wulongbei. Let me here thank the people who were kind enough to show us off from Andong Station. Among them was a young Chinese man by the name of Zhang Zemin whose mother was Japanese and who had been born in Nagasaki. Mr. Zhang worked as an employee of the lumber company and composed poems in Japanese.

WULONGBEI HOT SPRINGS

At 4:50 P.M. we arrived in Wulongbei, a quiet Chinese village. There were no Japanese living here outside of the staff at the station and at the hot springs inn, the Wulongge, located only about two hundred yards east of the station. In front one looked out onto the Sha River, and from behind rose the mountains. Nearby were paddy fields maintained, oddly enough, by the hot springs hotel, with frogs croaking and a thicket of trees reflected on the surface—the whole scene had a Japanese flavor to it. Two or three miles to the northwest, there floated up a mountain air tinged with purple, the distinctive character of a granite mountain known as Wulong Mountain. From the window where we were staying, we could see several stiff mountain peaks protruding loftily above the riverside willows of the Sha River, a landscape replete with majestic rock caves and overpowering beauty. The hot springs was discovered by chance by a company commander in the communications division who was stationed here at the time of the Sino-Japanese War. It is now indirectly managed by the South Manchurian Railway Company, and the bathing guests are primarily Japanese from Andong, as it has become a site frequented by Japanese traveling the An-Feng rail line. The source of the hot springs is pure alkali, and it is plentiful. We love hot springs and were wearing ourselves out traveling around to all the hot springs of Manchuria.

After bathing we walked aroung the Sha River. A remembrance of the setting sun over the willows wafted through, and the evening moon hung in the azure sky that had begun to clear from the light rain the previous day. Mr. Satō, who had brought his fishing gear with him from Japan, squatted down on the grass and fished for carp beneath the evening light. Among the poems my husband composed here was the following line:

> Fishing in the Sha River, the fish and the evening moon
> so dimly white.

The brick walls of the Wulongge were covered with ivy giving it the elegant external appearance of a country villa in France. Inside, the rooms were all purely Japanese, outfitted with steam heat from the hot springs in winter. The woman proprietor who was from Tokyo and the maids were gentle, quiet, agreeable women. When I arose here the next morning, in response to a request from the owner, I wrote a few lines of a poem, such as the following:

> The paddies and the grove of willows put the traveler
> in a frame of mind of returning home.

IMPRESSIONS OF FENGTIAN STATION

I set off from Wulongbei on the 8:32 A.M. train and arrived at Fengtian Station at 2:00 P.M. Inspired by Japan's dispatching troops to Shandong and the Jinan incident that erupted thereafter,[12] there was an anti-Japanese atmosphere emerging in the Three Eastern Provinces, and I wanted to visit a part of Inner Mongolia and northern Manchuria before it grew too heated. Thus, we visited Fengtian on the homeward journey.

We changed trains to one headed for Changchun from Dalian at 3:07 P.M., and before it departed we waited in the station-master's office. I received two letters there from Beijing. Reading them, I learned that disturbances in Beijing were increasing and that we would not be able to visit the capital. We had felt this already in Liaoyang and here were made to sense it even more acutely. The Fengtian Station was armed. Officers with squared shoulders coming and going with Japanese swords, the glint of agitated eyes, alarming movements of railway department staffers newly dispatched from the home office in Dalian the previous day, and the stationmaster's office in which we had rested turned into temporary army headquarters. I did not like the menacing spectacle unfolding, and when we left our room to wait for the train all manner of other foul news invaded my ears. When I consider the Sino-Japanese issue from the perspective of a Japanese, or when I try to consider it from the perspective of our neighbor the Chinese, or from my position as a citizen of the world, I cannot remain indifferent as these despicable bloodcurdling facts press in before my eyes. I imagine that Japan will end up isolated from the world, and it saddens me. This was precisely the time when the southern army was maintaining a superior position and the northern army of Zhang Xueliang [b. 1901] was forced to retreat beyond the Great Wall. I heard that with the force of a gust of wind the next day Japanese troops and railway employees would try to place the Jing-Feng rail line under guard and inspection. (When I asked later, though, I was very happy to learn that this was prevented from occurring through the desperate efforts of Fengtian Consul-General Hayashi and others).

We asked Fengtian Stationmaster Furuyama Katsuo about the safety of our traveling in the direction of Inner Mongolia, and he said, "It seems that Japanese women from many places have mostly withdrawn to Sipingjie, but I believe that if you do not stray too far from the rail line nor go too far into the interior, there is no real danger." Our guide, Mr. Katō Ikuya, also spent a short time collecting the views of workers in the Fengtian office of the South Manchurian Railway Company and said to us, "If we give up the idea of going from Zhengjiatun to Tongliao and instead travel only to Taonan and Qiqihar, there should be no trouble. In any event, we can get a better sense of the interior once we've reached Sipingjie." Mr. Satō the poet, loving the danger of it all, noted, "I'd be delighted to join you to Mongolia." My husband and I, though, had our misgivings about traveling to Mongolia, where there wasn't a single Japanese soldier because a certain incident necessitating the Japanese forces in Fengtian now be sent to China, and they might spark a second Jinan incident. I still, though, had this irrepressible desire to take a quick glimpse of Inner Mongolia, and without changing our plans we boarded a train at 3:15 P.M.

EN ROUTE TO SIPINGJIE

Unfortunately, we were unable to detrain at the intermediary station of Tieling. According to our guidebook, the city of Tieling lies to the south of the Chai River. The present city wall—with a circumference of about 2,800 yards and a height of some 20 feet—was built in the time of the Hongwu Emperor [fourteenth century] of the Ming dynasty. The thirteen-storey white pagoda at the Yuantong Temple in the city was famed for being founded in the second year of the Taihe reign (828) of the Tang dynasty. From the train we were also able to see an ancient pagoda at the Ciqing Temple on Mount Longshou to the east of the city. The Manchurian Flour Company managed by Japanese is well known here as a specialty industry with the best of prospects because of the abundance of wheat that grows in the area, and they apparently have factories in Changchun, Harbin, Jinan, Fengtian, Zhennanpu, and elsewhere. Also, making use of the broad expanses of low and damp land here at the delta of the Chai and Liao Rivers, over the past twenty years or more Korean immigrants have planted paddies with great success, and crop cultivation by Chinese, upon learning of the gains made by the Koreans, has increased dramatically. Paddy land management goes beyond this region, for from Muling and Modaoshi along the Chinese Eastern Railway to the east to Qiqihar in the west the surface area of land under cultivation, according to an investigation of 1924, came to 6,275 *mou* [about 1,046 acres], and the yield in unhulled rice came to about 335,000 bushels—and more is being planted now. The most important agricultural products of northern and southern Manchuria alike are soybeans, millet, sorghum, wheat, and corn—in that order—and 90 percent of local Chinese residents are involved in cultivating these crops. In northern Manchuria alone, they say that these cereal grains amount to some 60 percent of the freight carried in a given year by the Chinese Eastern Railway. With roughly thirty thousand Koreans having moved to northern Manchuria alone and working the paddy lands, the yield of rice will surely rise and may come to occupy an important position in the agricultural produce of Manchuria and Mongolia.

Next came Kaiyuan Station. I had heard that it was one of the major collection and distribution sites for Manchurian soybeans which had in recent years been exported as far away as European markets. We had observed soybeans at the Agricultural Experimentation Station we visited in Xiongyuecheng. The beans are generally divided into yellow, green, and black varieties, and then more finely separated into over two hundred kinds. The largest number were yellow beans which, in addition to being a food source, were pressed for oil that would be used for lighting and generally as an industrial resource. Its waste serves as fertilizer and as feed for domesticated animals. Four years ago the surface area of cultivated land in northern Manchuria was 1,450,000 *mou*, or about 14 percent of the entire surface area of northern Manchuria. Soybeans constitute the foremost crop planted here, and the expected harvest for 1925 is 1,309,510,000 bushels, and it seems to be expanding greatly. We passed through Changtu Station, but the city of Changtuxian, which was about five miles to the west of the station, was on the territory of the Mongolian Prince Bo [of the Khorchin Left Flank Rear Banner]. It had been opened by Chinese from the Jiaqing reign period of the Qing dynasty in the early nineteenth century. The Mongolian prince had apparently set up a regional office here and collected a land rent. On a mountain two miles to the north at Manjing Station, we saw a memorial tablet erected at the site of the truce treaty between the Japanese and Russian armies. After the great battle at Fengtian, Japanese cavalrymen had pursued the Russian troops as far as Changtu before the war ended.

SIPINGJIE

We arrived in Sipingjie at 6:19 P.M. and put up at the Japanese inn, the Uenaka, in front of the station. The rain that apparently fell on the Yalu River yesterday fell here as well. Sipingjie was a new city that had emerged because of the opening of the main line of the Manchurian railway. It was opened to traffic the year before last when the Si-Tao rail line made it a terminus, and as it had become the most important gateway, coming or going, for goods from various sites in Inner Mongolia and

Manchuria, both the Chinese city and the Japanese city had grown rapidly. The merchandise sent from this station was largely millet, about seventy thousand tons each year, accounting for one-third of the entire amount of millet exported from all of Manchuria. According to reports Mr. Katō consulted at the South Manchurian Railway office and elsewhere, he confirmed that evening that all Japanese women from various sites in Inner Mongolia along the Si-Tao rail line had withdrawn to Sipingjie or in the Dalian direction. I learned that if we traveled on daytime trains, there was no danger, and we decided to take a train the following morning that went directly to Taonan in Inner Mongolia. The Chinese railway office of the Si-Tao line sent a first-class bus for three men, but they said that there was no precedent for a woman, so I alone purchased a ticket. We were told that it was too dangerous to leave in the evening, so we cut short our sightseeing in Sipingjie. We left the dimly lit Uenaka bath house, and, listening to the rain, retired early that evening, feeling very isolated.

OFF TO INNER MONGOLIA

We left Sipingjie on a 7:00 A.M. train the next morning, the 25th, and gradually began to see a section of the hinterland of Inner Mongolia. Not only in the Sipingjie area but the terrain of Mongolia from Fengtian north through all that we passed on the trunk line of the South Manchurian Railway, both following the mountains and spanning the rivers, was frequently low, damp, and fertile land. Ever since the late Qing period, Chinese had moved to the area and been cultivating newly opened land. Thus, elm and willow trees were growing luxuriantly, and one could see greenery in the fields and on the hillsides. When we had gone some five miles to the west of Sipingjie, the four directions all along the railway line became a wide open, flat sandy plain without a single tree in sight. Looking through a telescope, I could see here and there on the edge of the horizon villages with a few houses in them and along the few roads crisscrossing through the sand a group of travelers with horse- and ox-drawn carts formed a thin dotted line. Grasslands were few and far between on the sand. Occasionally, where there was grass growing, it lacked the early summer color of youth- fulness because of the sandy dust. The grass here appeared stunted with a look of soda. As I stared out at this desolate and lonely world of sand, for the first time I felt as though I was taking my first step into the interior of Mongolia.

Changing trains from the one we had taken until the previ- ous day, we boarded, again as nonpaying passengers, under the armed guard of Chinese officers and soldiers. They took seats in our compartment, chatting amiably though rudely and snack- ing all the while. Numerous armed Chinese soldiers and patrols were guarding every station en route. In addition to the four of us, there was only one other Japanese passenger, all the rest on board being Chinese. I saw among them several Manchu men and women and Mongolian men in Han Chinese dress. Com- pared to the peace of mind we had enjoyed on board trains un- til the previous day when all of the station attendants, guard troops, and patrols had been Japanese, the spectacle surround- ing us now suddenly changed, and I felt a certain unease and marvel, as though we had been chased into a world of people we did not know. Everything was still OK, because it was a daytime train, but if it had been nightime, I'd probably have felt rather lonely.

The stations along the rail line were all separated from the cities and villages, there being only Western-style brick build- ings attached to each station. All manner of large and small carts were assembled at every station to transport produce.

There were numerous sorts of carts being used by both Chinese and Mongolians, like the numerous ideographs found under "cart" in Chinese dictionaries. The two most numerous were the "big-headed" cart and the "double-large" cart, which, because of their firm structures, carried between five hundred and one thousand catties of produce over any sort of difficult road. The wheels did not use spokes, but they simply crossed three thick pieces of wood—looking like the Japanese syllabary symbol *ki*—within the wheel frame. There might be anywhere from four or five to as many as ten horses attached to pull these carts because they were transporting such a large quantity of merchandise along roads far and near. Oxen and mules were mixed in among the horses, but they were limited to comparatively more proximate distances. There were also "white" carts pulled by two or three head of oxen only. These carts were laden with five to six hundred catties of produce, and carts laden with two to three hundred catties of produce drawn by a single ox were called pulley carts. One-wheeled handcarts or wheelbarrows were also used to carry small cargo within the cities and villages. Horse-drawn carts known as palanquins, used for transporting people, were also employed, and we saw not a single rickshaw in Inner Mongolia. These palanquins were more often pulled by mules than by horses. What they did was to place a sedan chair on top of a cart; those carrying an official or wealthy person were one-horse carriages and were rather beautifully decorated, while unadorned palanquins for use over great distances were called dry land carts and were pulled by two or three mules. The speed such palanquins could make was said to be thirty to forty miles per day.

I felt a certain sense of joy looking at these carts at every station. Among the pack animals used for hauling produce were camels, mules, and donkeys, and camels were most prevalent in the western part of Inner Mongolia. Along the train line we traveled, we didn't see a single camel, and I was as disappointed as a little child. A smattering of trees had been transplanted at the train stations, all willows. We did also see a few vegetable fields near the stations, and there were pigs and ducks making merry there, probably to be used for food for the Chinese station attendants.

Among the stations en route, Bamiancheng was said to be terrain opened early on by Han Chinese with a population that had reached twenty thousand Chinese, but we were unable to see it from the station. Sanjiangkou on the right bank of the Liao River was well known as a commercial city to which junks sailed from Yingkou. Zhengjiatun was a commercial city under the jurisdiction of Liaoyuan county. Han Chinese cultivation was flourishing at the delta of the Liao River, and a branch rail line had recently opened from this station to Tongliao (Bayantaria) about one hundred miles to the northwest. There was a famous Lama temple in Tongliao, and about twelve miles to the north of it was the residence of the Darkhan Wang [of the Khorchin Left Flank Middle Banner], one of the Mongolian princes. Under normal circumstances, we would have changed to the Zheng-Tong line and taken it there, but we had to abandon that notion. Sanmiancheng, Sanjiangkou, and Zhengjiatun were all too far from the station for us to see.

We ate the lunch boxes we had brough along with us. A steward several times handed us damp, wrung out towels and poured us tea on several occasions as well, though when I pondered what water had been used to make it, I had an uneasy feeling about it. I noticed among the sweets the steward was selling throughout the train that many of them were of the

Morinaga brand. The cigarettes and lemon pop were both Chinese brands. I was delighted to see that Mr. Morinaga's business had grown to Manchuria and Mongolia.

———

The dividing lines between the domains of the various Mongolian princes were indicated by piling small stones up high and then standing up tree branches in them. These are known as *obo* and are regarded as sacred, to be prayed to as the deity of the land. Every year a number of religious festivals are carried out surrounding them at which Mongolian men and women sing and dance. At mountain passes in Japan, stones are piled up and draw ropes are stretched out, and these seem to have a religious, ethnographic relationship to being seen as a deity and being prayed to. Thanks to Mr. Katō's attentiveness, we were able to see an *obo* on two occasions from a distance. As the sandy terrain proceeded inland along the rail line, we came upon places where hills of sand had swelled up in waves, and several times the *obo* that I was trying to see through a telescope were blocked from view by these sand hills.

TAONAN

That afternoon, we grew tired of the monotony of the vista from the train window, which looked out onto sand and more sand. Everyone picked up a notebook and composed a poem—Mr. Satō wrote a haiku—and at 3:30 P.M. we reached that day's objective of Taonan. Before we arrived, Mr. Katō pointed out to us the city of Taonan from the window on the left side of the train. It was unlike the other cities—Jinzhou, Xiongyuecheng, Liaoyang, and the like—that we had seen thus far; the city walls and all the homes in Taonan were all precisely the same ashen color, for these were fortified earthen ramparts made by piling up sand in the desert into the shape of a square of about thirty-six hundred yards to a side. The sun was setting just then, and it shone on one section of the wall, enabling us to see our approach to the city, but it was a cloudy day and that made it difficult to distinguish sand from the earthen walls—it seemed like a natural camouflage vis-à-vis an enemy. The light gray wall, which on this barren field of sand lacked so much as a single tree to hint at detail—this may have been a destroyed town from antiquity, but it was now a prosperous new city recently constructed. Ever since climbing Qianshan, my husband had been writing Japanese and Chinese poems, and he wrote the following work [in Chinese] reflecting his impressions at this time:

> Traveling together for thousands of miles,
> Two friends and one poetess wife.
> We have boarded trains as if they were our home,
> Sitting across from one another with our minuscule
>   verses.
> The road enters eastern Mongolia, sand and sky
>   together,
> The winds blows the yellow dust, darkening in the
>   mist,
> Suddenly from the train window we see the earthen
>   ramparts clearly,
> Rays of the sun beaming on the city of Taonan.

One inconvenient thing was that when the train arrived in Taonan Station, we were isolated in a area over a mile to the north of the city of Taonan. We were met by some people from the local South Manchurian Railway office and boarded a lovely horse-drawn carriage they supplied. There were all manner of

Chinese carts and wagons in the area as well as filthy Russian-style covered wagons for carrying passengers. It was late May, and the temperature in the sand was such that I needed to use a fan. Each of the four city walls—east, west, south, and north—had two gates, a large one and a small one. We entered the city through the large eastern gate used by most people. Several armed Chinese soldiers guarded each gate. A number of ferocious tartar dogs—commonly known as Mongolian dogs—wandered about and began barking when they saw the foreigners. In the mixture of Chinese and Mongolian dress, a gray sand storm whirled up with great density amid all the many different carts and wagons. We call it sand, but it was of a very fine clay quality. Virtually all the homes inside the city were of simple construction whose roof and walls were fortified by refining this sand. Here and there one saw a few grand brick buildings built for official use along the bustling main streets.

We first went to the office of the South Manchurian Railway and met its director, Mr. Nishimura Kiyoshi. We learned from Mr. Nishimura that the local anti-Japanese climate had in fact not grown tense to the point of danger. As a precaution against every eventuality, though, all Japanese women resident there had been evacuated, and only the male personnel from the South Manchurian Railway office remained. Mr. Nishimura took us out onto the roof of his office and offered us a detailed explanation of the city from our bird's-eye view. He also showed us a Mongolian dwelling, a yurt—known as a *bao* in Chinese—in the garden. This one had been given to his office by a certain Mongolian prince and appeared to be representative of the home of an aristocrat. Being a nomadic people, the Mongolians were always pursuing land with water and grass.

There were two kinds of yurt: a convenient, movable form for dismantling and transporting, and a firm semipermanent form with earthen walls and thatched roof for those Mongolians who, while stationary, lived on terrain abundant in water and grass—such as the southeastern portion of the Xing'an Mountains—having somewhat transformed the originally movable style of yurt. From the outside both had the form of a circular tent. The one in the garden of the South Manchurian Railway office was a movable yurt—perhaps thirteen or fourteen feet high to the pinnacle of the dwelling, seven or eight feet in circumference in its cylindrical portion, and less than twenty square yards of space at the base.[13] When you examine its overall structure from inside, you can separate the roof from the cylindrical part, with the former sitting on top of the latter. The roof was constructed of rounded pieces of willow in the form of an umbrella and freely opened and closed by fastening the windlass at the apex with a rope made of cowhide. The inside of the windlass had a cross-shaped spindle, and it formed a circular window for lighting as well as for releasing smoke. A carpet covering this window worked by means of a string mechanism to allow or prevent light from entering from the outside. Also, the framework of the cylindrical base was built by connecting it to a lattice of four willow branches roughly one inch in diameter. The entranceway always facing southeast was about 3.5 feet high, about 2.5 feet wide, and opened only in a specific place. The exterior of the yurt with its roof and surrounding cylindrical base was wrapped in two layers of rough but sturdy carpet made of wool. That is why the Chinese called it a *bao*, or "wrapping." To prevent the rugs from peeling off, they used cords made of camel hair that were coiled and tied from top to bottom and left to right around the exterior of the yurt. To the entrance was attached a double small door or, in place of a door, a carpet curtain was lowered. It was a primitive structure overall in which not a single nail had been used, and one could easily take it apart or reassemble it.

Inside, all the wood of the frame was painted red tinged with black. Although this yurt was empty, there is a specific internal apparatus Mongolians use when they actually live in one. They lay carpets on all sides of the dirt floor, use a wooden chest set directly inside from the entranceway and a little to the left as an altar, place a Buddhist image and a photo of the Living Buddha, the dharma king of Lamaism, upon it, line up some Buddhist altar equipment, say prayers in the morning and evening, and do not turn their feet in their sleep. To the left of the altar is a seat for a man, and a guest may sit there as well. To the right is a female seat, and various items are placed there: water cisterns, foodstuffs, kitchen items, and large and small chests into which are placed valuables and clothing. Placing the superior position to the left is the same as in ancient Japanese temples. In the center, right on the dirt floor, they set up a stove and a basket of cow manure they dry for fuel; there they do their cooking and build a fire to generate heat. On a table next to the entrance on the right are laid out tea utensils and milking equipment, and to the right they bring in infant cattle and sheep to protect them in mid-winter. Four or five people can sleep in a single yurt, and they sleep on their sides on top of the carpets with their clothing as bedding. Poor people simply sleep with their clothes on. The yurts are frequently dismantled, moved, and rebuilt on sand near grassland; thus, they are relatively clean and smell of mutton and the milk of cattle and sheep. They say that, unlike the Chinese, they don't mind the smell. In the nomadic areas, the Mongolian princes apparently also live in yurts, and princes and nobles divide their families into several groups to that end.

I listened to Mr. Nishimura's explanation of the yurt, and

then in the immense area under the auspices of the South Man-churian Railway Company office we were shown fields in which they were attempting to produce flowers and agricultural pro-duce suitable to Mongolia. Later, with the guidance of a South Manchurian Railway Company staff member we rode in the office carriage on a tour of the city.

▭ ▮ ▭

Mongolia is divided into Inner Mongolia and Outer Mongo-lia, and Inner Mongolia alone covers roughly 450,000 square miles (Japan's total surface area is 259,877 square miles). We had now come to Taonan in the northeastern part of Inner Mongolia, on the southern shore of the Taor River. The great Xing'an Mountain range separating Inner and Outer Mongo-lia was hidden beneath the horizon far away and all we could see was vast, endless desert terrain. Mongolia specialists say, "You'll never get an accurate sense of Mongolia unless you visit both Inner and Outer Mongolia." I imagine there's little doubt about it. In particular, I remember twenty-five years ago reading Dr. Naka Michiyo's [1851–1908] famous work, *Chingisu kan jitsuroku* (The Veritable Record of Chinggis Khan), a translation of the *Yuanchao bishi* (Secret History of the Mongols);[14] it gave me insight into the immense place that Mongolia was seven hundred years ago. Fifteen years ago I read *Higashi Mōko* (Eastern Mongolia), edited by the Guan-dong Governor-General's office, and it only touched on the contemporary human geography of Inner Mongolia. I once skimmed *Mōko ryokō* (Travels in Mongolia), published in the late Meiji period by Dr. Torii Ryūzō, but was unable to read it more carefully. This was the poor extent of the preparatory information I had acquired about Mongolia. Having actually seen and had personal contact with the wind and ways of one part of this locale, the concrete reliability of actually experiencing all this was far more gratifying than hearing about it one thousand times. In so doing, I had also acquired a basis for imagining what conditions in Outer Mongolia might be like.

According to the autonomous administrative units, the Inner Mongolian region was divided overall into four parts: the four Eastern Leagues (Jirim League with four tribes distributed in ten banners, Josotu League with two tribes distributed in five banners, Juu Uda League with eight tribes distributed in eleven banners, and Shili-yin Gool League with five tribes distributed in ten banners), the two Western Leagues (Ulaanchab League with four tribes distributed in six banners and Yekhe Juu League with one tribe distributed in seven banners), Guihua cheng Tümed, and Chakhar with eight banners. Mongolia has retained since antiquity a system of ethnic chieftains, and the head of each grouping is called a *jasag* (C. *zhasake*). There are three kinds of jasag: prince (*wang*), duke (*güng* [C. *gong*]), and gentry (*taiji*), all of them hereditary. When there is no heir, a successor is selected by the relatives of the prince, duke, or gentry. These jasag are all descendents of Emperor Taizu of the Yuan dynasty—namely Chinggis Khan [1162–1227]; everyone in the Josotu League alone was a descendent of sons-in-law and chief vassals of Chinggis. There were several jasag, and first among them was chief. One of the Qing dynasty's appeasement policies was to award others the ranks of prince, duke, and gentry. The tribal group each governed by a jasag was called a banner (*qi*), and several banners came together into a league (*meng*). Each league had a league chief and an assistant league chief; the Qing emperor chose men of older age and high moral stature among the jasag, and every three years the league leader summoned the various banners under his authority and convened a meeting of leagues much like a diet. Since the founding of the

Republic of China [in 1912], however, league leaders have no longer been selected and diets no longer convened.

Although the jasag were called princes and dukes, in reality they were little more than ancient tribal chieftains. Some among them controlled domains as large as six hundred square miles. On small territories in the desolate wilderness, they were unable to advance beyond their station of nomad chief ruling over the grazing life of family members and fellow clan members, and they had no savings accumulated. They had a "princely residence," a "land bureau" that collected land rents on terrain reclaimed by Han Chinese migrants, and an "office of military affairs" of troops to deal with bandits—all of these were extremely rudimentary and rough facilities. By contrast, their Lamaist temples were of comparatively fine architecture. While the land was the dominion of the princes and dukes, from the late Qing period Han Chinese had been continuously migrating into the area, and especially in recent years their numbers have been rising sharply. The administrative power over the land released to these Chinese who pay a land rent has not been extended to the Chinese, and this authority remains in the hands of the government. That is, on land opened up to Han Chinese migrants, the Chinese government has newly set up county administrations and placed them under the control of the various provinces contiguous to this region, thus retaining jurisdiction over the Han Chinese. Only the Mongolians living on this opened land have princes and dukes with administrative power, though in recent years these Mongolians have lost their pasture lands to Han Chinese, and, unable to sustain a struggle for existence, they have been gradually drifting further inland to unopened terrain.

Taonan, where we had arrived that day, was on terrain known in Mongolian as *shaajagai modu* (C. *shajijie maotu*) that was part of the domain (over 1,070 square miles) of the banner of the princely estate of the jasag of Jirim League of the four Eastern Leagues. Taonan was the terminus of the Si-Tao rail line, lying 190 miles to the southwest of Sipingjie. This terrain was first opened in the 28th year of the reign of the Guangxu emperor (1902) of the late Qing dynasty, when it was given the Chinese name of Shuangliuzhen; at the time it was a small station of some forty households of Han Chinese immigrants. Two years later, the Russo-Japanese War broke out, and as the demand for domestic animals increased it rapidly developed as a collection and distribution center for animal husbandry. The following year, 1905, the Chinese government renamed it Taonan and established Taonan prefecture. In 1913, the prefecture was abolished and replaced by Taonan county, and a government office and military troops as parts of a county office were put into place. It it now part of Fengtian province.

We toured the sights of the city of Taonan by horse-drawn carriage. Facing the large gates in each of the four city walls, four boulevards in a grid pattern were marked out, and in addition twelve east-west streets and six north-south streets crisscrossed, forming a new, orderly city. It was divided into 135 blocks, and while the northern half of the city was densely populated, the southern half had empty areas in it. However, it will only take three or four more years before Han Chinese households fill up this space. The opening of the rail line has made Taonan a strategic center for produce distribution, and they expect that it will be flourishing more and more in the future. Chinese who peddle wares from Fengtian into various sites in Inner Mongolia by wagon and tent are said to be primarily merchants from Zhengjiatun. We noted large-scale merchant houses—among them general stores with textiles, grain merchants, liquor manufacturing, pelt and hide merchants, transport companies, inns, and restaurants. The present Han Chinese population has reached forty-five thousand. In addition, there are seven hundred Koreans and only about thirty Japanese. Aside from a drugstore, Japanese merchants have apparently established no major works here as yet.

Fat licorice ten feet long is harvested at certain places in Mongolia. I heard that Japanese who hire patient Chinese to extract it from the sand and then corner the market in it have gained a foothold here and in Zhengjiatun and have proceeded further inland. Inasmuch as they carry cash with them, there's a danger that they will be attacked by bandits. Some Chinese merchants travel in groups and others trade in kind and thus carry little cash; all of them are conversant in Mongolian and know Mongolian customs and practices. This lessens the danger of bandit attacks and indeed brings them closer to the Mongolian people. Insofar as Japanese lack these preconditions, they lack the stoic strength and the industrial and frugal mindset of the Chinese. They are also weaker in group cohesion, and when they go overseas and find themselves excluded, they isolatedly attempt to secure profit. This is one major weakness in which Japanese merchants cannot compete with their Chinese counterparts in Manchuria and Mongolia. Several external reasons for this come to mind: Japanese do not have leaseholds on land, the Chinese police are incapable of protecting foreigners, there are no Chinese banks in which they can place their trust, the Chinese currency system is in chaos, and there are effectively no health facilities in the interior of Manchuria and Mongolia. However, while the Chinese do have leases on land, they are confronted by all the other difficulties and dangers that they cannot avoid, and with each passing year these problems are growing. Furthermore, while subject to all of this maltreatment in recent years, over one million Koreans have flooded into Manchuria and Mongolia. They have already produced considerable results for their labors in cultivated paddy lands and the like. I must lament the lax nature of the Japanese spirit of adventure and hard work.

Walking around the streets of Taonan, we saw a Chinese rural theater in an empty lot in front of the local Guandi Temple.[15] It struck me as precisely at the level of festival music one sees in rituals in the environs of Tokyo; even the shape of the tent they worked from was similar. I don't know what this theater was called, but two military commanders faced each other on a table and were fighting over something. Glasses were thrown. Their lines were delivered in verse. We had planned to visit Beijing and take in some theater there, but those plans had been abandoned, so I was happy to have had this glimpse even of rural theater. I did, though, feel quite strange when crowds of Chinese people and Chinese troops were staring at me in my Western dress.

Originally, the reason that Mongolians called this place *shaajagai modu* had to do with the fact that there was one old elm tree there oddly in the sand, and it was the goal in transport across the plain. Thus, they used the Mongolian word *shaajagai modu*, meaning elm tree, as the local place name. Literally translated it would mean "magpie tree," as the Mongolians dubbed this elm a tree upon which magpies alighted. Until recently the tree was flourishing, but it has now died and, as a remembrance, is regarded as sacred. They have built a wall around it to prevent people from approaching too closely. I peeped in at the dead tree from a crevice in the wall. A noted sight here, it is featured on a picture postcard, too.

The Taor River flows directly in front of one of the gates

to the city. One can see the greenery of low willow trees and summer grass from its shore. The Nen River [length: 425 miles] begins to the southwest of Mount Yilehuli in the great Xing'an range which forms the border with Outer Mongolia, and then flows to the southeast, north of Mergen [C. Moliugen] and west of Qiqihar. It then enters the terrain of the Dörbed [C. Du'erbodu] tribe of Inner Mongolia, flows to the southeast as far as Sanjiangkou, and then meets up with the Sungari River. One of its tributaries is the Taor River. I was reminded of a line from a poem, *Congjun xing* (Travels with the Army), by the Tang-period poet Wang Changling:

> Earlier the army had fought an evening battle north of
> the Tao River,
> I reported the taking of the Tuguhun alive.

When you imagine the Tuguhun, a branch of the ancient Xianbi people from Liaodong, fighting with Han Chinese troops in this area and being taken alive, you sense in an eerie way the approach of historical events of two thousand years ago. Standing on the banks of the river, I looked out on the far shore at the uncanny spectacle of the color of the sun as it was about to descend into the horizon of pure sand. The idea of an age-old, penetrating sense of loneliness and sorrow one finds in the great Chinese poets, like Li Bo [701–62], struck me as something with extremely profound roots. I had the feeling that the essence of Chinese literature had not been understood by Edo-period Japanese specialists in Chinese literature who had not actually seen this scenery of the north.

We stayed at the only Japanese hotel, the Datong Inn, which was managed under a Chinese name. One young housewife remained there, having not evacuated with the others, and she treated us kindly. Coming in from the sandy dust, we were only too happy to be able to bathe in hot water. We had no alternative but to forbear the poor quality of the well water, among other things. We came prepared with canned food to eat, but to our surprise we were able to dine that evening on Japanese cuisine like that in inns back home—the whole thing seemed sort of wasteful to me. They said it was unsafe just now, so they tightly locked the door of the inn at sunset. After dinner, Mr. Satō Sōnosuke roused Mr. Katō and they went for a walk. We stayed back at the inn and talked with Mr. Mori Tatena. Mr. Mori was in charge of the commissary for the South Manchurian Railway Company in Sipingjie, and he was on his way home from a business trip for the company into Mongolia. Having met us, he decided to postpone his departure that evening by a day. When he had earlier lived in Tokyo, he used to recite poetry, and we learned from conversation that he knew Yoshii Yū, among others. He was also close to our old friend in Dalian, Nishida Inosuke. We were both pleased to have stopped at the same inn overnight as Mr. Mori far off in the wilderness of Mongolia. More than anything, his recitation of poems brought him closer to us.

While we were learning about life in Mongolia from Mr. Mori, Satō and Katō returned with looks of great astonishment on their faces. They had heard that there was a single Japanese woman on some back street of the town, and the young poet Katō tried to pay her a visit, but she had locked her door well before. When they tried to rouse her and for a short time spoke with her inside her home, suddenly they heard two gun shots and loud human noises. The two men returned having lost all color in their faces. That evening the dreams of our party of four were all disquieting. Since we had been told to avoid, at all cost, the possibility of being attacked by a mob or bandits, we slept with the lights inside purposefully extinguished.

ON BOARD ALONG THE TAO-ANG LINE

The following morning, my husband rose early and watched the sun rise over the desert. After breakfast, a carriage arrived for us from the South Manchurian Railway office, and we rode to Taonan Station on the Tao-Ang rail line one mile to the northwest. We boarded an 8:00 A.M. train headed for Ang'angxi. This line was the most recently completed Chinese railway; with capital financing from the South Manchurian Railway Company, construction had been completed in South Manchurian Railway hands. We learned from Mr. Katō that during construction they had been inundated by flood waters, and en route we saw a lake that had come into existence as a result of the flood. This lake that had emerged just three years earlier would likely not dry up for another fifty years. Natural phenomena in a huge country occur on a huge scale. The train was traveling from Taonan to the west-northwest. The desert was even more barren than the previous day, and we scarely saw a single dwelling save the buildings at the train stations along the rail line.

Dongping, a small station on the Tao-Ang line, was, from the perspective of the administrative zones of the Chinese government, the boundary between Fengtian province and Heilongjiang province. On the eastern side of the Xing'an range, also in Mongolia, this area where the two provinces met in the delta of the Nen River seemed like a quiet region conducive to working new land by immigrants: with the Xing'an Mountains serving as a barrier, they were protected somewhat from the ferocious sandstorms of Outer Mongolia that blew through with mighty northwest winds; the topography gradually sloped to the southeast and discharged the soda from the soil; and everytime rivers from the Xing'an Mountains flooded, they brought in organic matter that served as natural fertilizer. In the distant past, in addition to Mongolians, the Tungusic people crossed the Xing'an Mountains and developed this large area, but in 1583 (the eleventh year of the Tenshō reign period in Japan) the Manchus first used troops against these tribes of people. In the reign of the Shunzhi emperor of the Qing dynasty [r. 1644–61], it was completely conquered and has now become Heilongjiang province. I learned that the Tungusic people quickly escaped into the delta of the Amur River, and the Mongolians there now belong to the various princes and dukes of the banners of Dörbed, Jalaid (C. Zhalaite), and Gorlos (C. Guo'erluosi) in Jirim League; many of their landowners have forty to fifty hectares, and there are even some with as much as two thousand hectares, sixty head of cattle and horses, and over four hundred head of sheep. The land of these Mongolians is pasture land, but since the Qing era land has been forcibly opened for cultivation by virtue of the intrusion of Han Chinese. Each year the amount of such land increases, and on the somewhat less than four thousand square miles of the Jalaid banner's domain alone, they account for 70 percent of the total land holdings. Han Chinese were growing varieties of sorghum, Chinese millet, foxtail millet, buckwheat, corn, hemp, melons, green beans, and red beans. In recent years, we were told, Koreans had begun planting rice as tenant farmers, but inasmuch this was all being done in the river deltas, we could not see anything that looked like fertile soil from our vantage point on the train.

ANG'ANGXI STATION

We arrived at Ang'angxi, the northern terminus of the Tao-Ang line, at 4:00 P.M. The owner of the Angrong Hotel, the only Japanese inn there, had come to meet us with a car from the city of Ang'angxi, as the station was four miles removed from the city. The city had taken shape because Ang'angxi Station was on the Chinese Eastern Railway and because it was close to Qiqihar, the capital of Heilongjiang province. Russians connected with the railway lived there together with Chinese. The railroad was now a Sino-Russian joint venture, and there were numerous Russian-style buildings in the city insofar as the railway had been administered under the eastern advance of the Russian Empire before the Russo-Japanese War. The Angrong Hotel was one such edifice. In May of 1912, I had taken a train from Vladivostok, and I recall that en route to Manzhouli we passed through this station at dawn of the second day. I was traveling all by myself at that time, and compared to the loneliness of not seeing another Japanese in the train compartments, this time I had fellow travelers and the South Manchurian Railway poet Mr. Katō in particular was seeing to our needs with meticulous attention and kindness. We could not but rejoice in the fact that everywhere we went people were waiting for us.

QIQIHAR

Over the sixty miles between Ang'angxi and Qiqihar, the capital of Heilongjiang province, the Chinese government had laid a narrow-gauge railway, the Qi-Ang line. The train operated twice a day, morning and evening. We put our bags in the hotel, and immediately hired a car to take us to the capital. Although it was 5:00 P.M., the sun was still high in the sky in late May. The road, as usual, was covered with sand, and the dust carried by the wind bounced off the car all in white. As we went nearby certain sandy knolls, our Japanese driver told us that a group of bandits had been killed by Chinese troops near there. When the Chinese government apprehended bandits, they usually just executed them without a trial. Thus, he noted, bandits carried out acts of great brutality so as not to leave any criminal evidence behind.

We proceeded to visit Mr. Hayakawa Masao, director of the South Manchurian Railway Company office in the outskirts of Qiqihar. There was a magnificent automobile parked at the entrance to the office, and several Chinese soldiers were standing around it. I learned that a high Chinese official was paying a visit. When I presented my name card, both Mr. Hayakawa and his wife greeted us and said that they had been waiting for us to arrive. Abandoning a punctilious, formal greeting as though this were not the first meeting, he said, "Perfect timing. The wife of Wu Junsheng is here right now. Let me introduce you." And he led us into his parlor. There we saw two Chinese ladies dressed elegantly. One was the second wife, surnamed Li, of Wu Junsheng, commissioner of Heilongjiang province; the other was the wife, surnamed Ma, of Lieutenant General Liu Dequan, who was superintendent-general of the police of this province and simultaneously held several other important posts. I was quickly seated between these two women, and with Mr. and Mrs. Hayakawa's assistance as interpreters, our conversation covered many different topics. Mr. Wu's wife originally hailed from Beijing; she was both intelligent and full of emotion. Particularly since marrying Mr. Wu, she had yearned for the new knowledge of the world, had paid attention to

women's education, and seemed seriously concerned with social reform and aid to the poor. Her stature was attested to by
the fact that local people said of her, "In Heilongjiang province
there are two warlords. One is the husband Mr. Wu and one is
his wife." A warlord was the local ruler who held all effective
power. Mr. Wu's love for his wife was profound, and she loved
and respected him as well. If Mr. Wu, who was over seventy
years of age, were to die, she was resigned to committing sui-
cide and following him in death. They say that for some time
past two coffins had been prepared at the Wu estate in Qiqihar.
She was twenty-seven years old and her Chinese beauty had an
extraordinary youthfulness about it.

Liu's wife seemed to me a bit older but with the same
youthful appearance. Her husband had early on graduated
from the Military Academy in Japan, while she had studied in
Tokyo and was conversant in Japanese. In her wisdom, enthusiasm, and education in the new learning, she seemed a fine
match for her husband. Because I had not had the opportunity
since coming to Manchuria and Mongolia to meet an educated
Chinese woman, this chance meeting was especially providen-
tial. The ladies asked about how Ms. Takenaka Shigeko of the
Tōkyō asahi shinbun (Tokyo Daily News) was faring. A few
year back, Ms. Takenaka had visited this region and spoken
with these ladies. Since we had come into the parlor, I noticed
something taking place. A young girl of some twelve or thirteen years of age attired in a bright reddish brown Chinese
dress about three feet from Mrs. Wu stood erect, immobile.
From her green eyes and white complexion, I could see at a
glance that she was not Chinese. According to Mrs. Hayakawa,
Mrs. Wu had taken pity on her, a Russian orphan after the
Revolution of 1917, and made her a serving girl. The girl was
holding a beautiful box under her left arm, and when Mrs. Wu
bid her, she took a long, thin cigarette from the box and lit it for

her. She then resumed her erect, immobile pose. It struck me as somewhat odd that this might be something of which elite women in China would be proud.

A NIGHT ON THE NEN RIVER

Before nightfall we walked around the city of Qiqihar and visited the Japanese consulate. We were then to board the evening train to return to Ang'angxi. A late night train at 2:50 A.M. was scheduled for Harbin. When we mentioned this, in an effort to leave the South Manchurian Railway office, Mrs. Wu interupted and invited us to Mrs. Liu's river villa outside the city; it would add to the interest of this trip for us as poets. In fact, she wanted us to join her back at her residence, as her husband was on a visit to Beijing and she wanted to show us the scenery of the Nen River. Our plans did not allow for this, and when we refused she encouraged us further, saying that she would see that a special train was arranged for us to go to Ang'angxi late in the night and by all means we should now go to the river villa. Mr. and Mrs. Hayakawa as well as Mrs. Liu enthusiastically encouraged us, too, and eventually we accepted their kindness and separated, with the men driving in Mr. Hayakawa's car and Mrs. Hayakawa and me driving with the two ladies.

Entering the city of Qiqihar, we passed through a lively market, and we then left through a gate on the other side of town. After a while we arrived at Lieutenant General Liu's villa on the bank of the Nen River at dusk. A group of soldiers guarding the front gate suddenly under orders from their officer stunned us by lining up on either side and presenting arms. Either Mrs. Hayakawa or Mr. Katō whispered, "They're saluting you as guests of the lady warlord." I felt myself blushing unawares. The villa was a one-storey, Western-style structure with a chic salon facing the river. A garden had been built in the courtyard surrounded by four walls, but none of the trees had yet blossomed flowers, as the difference in the northern temperature had been taken into account. Perhaps because she had arranged it by telephone from the South Manchurian Railway office, her husband, Mr. Liu Dequan, arrived before us and was there to welcome us. He spoke Japanese quite well, and he was a lieutenant general, a man of intelligence in the prime of life who was greatly respected by warlord Wu Junsheng. Mrs. Wu guided us walking down to the river, and it was marvelous to stand before the Nen River, this immense waterway of Mongolia. In the extraordinarily white sand at the water's edge, pebbles were scattered about in a wide array of magnificent colors; agate was mixed in among them, like the seashore at Aikawa on Sado Island that I visited several years earlier. The sun had already sunk in the distance at the edge of the sand by the river, and the afterglow tinged in purplish red was reflecting on the water, illuminating the sand on the river bank and basking our group in colors as we sauntered along. In particular, the white visages of Mrs. Wu and Mrs. Liu among us, their silk coats with silver thread on a deep turquoise background, a slender hand picking up agate seemed to float up to me—it was a beautiful sight. The two young men, Satō and Katō, walked along intent on collecting agate. Two moored vessels, as per orders from her husband, were waiting for us at the shore. A crescent moon eerily added light of a jade-green color to the afterglow of the setting sun, as several wild geese heading north passed by crying out. The men boarded one of the moored vessels, with Mr. Liu taking the oar, while we women boarded the other boat, and Mrs. Wu paddled. There was no wind and the sky was clear, a beautiful calm evening in which no thought of the sandy world of Mongolia occurred whatsoever. The two boats floated on the crystal clear water and silently carried us to a sandbar in the river. There stood a grove of luxuriant young willow trees. We stepped onto the island from the boat and walked in among the riverside willows, as small birds were startled and took wing. Listening to their cries reminded me of the reed warblers in Japan. My husband learned from Mr. Liu that the Chinese name for this bird is *weique*, and I was happy to know that the two countries' names naturally coincided in their relationship to "reeds."

Although the willow trees were young, they were so tall that everyone disappeared in their overgrowth. While leaning on a willow branch, I looked up at the jade-green moon for awhile. Again wild geese cried out as they flew by. At Mrs. Hayakawa's urging, we returned to the boats, and with a bunch of willow branches that she had broken off herself, Mrs. Wu got on board and placed the branches on either side of the boat. I was delighted to the point of tears to find that women of such elegance in war-torn China still existed. The sky was golden flecks of stars inlaid on a deep ultramarine, and already by late May the Milky Way was thickly flowing with milk. On the boat, the moon and the shimmering of clear water made the turquoise overcoats of Mrs. Wu and Mrs. Liu appear white. Again, the straightforward Mrs. Wu took the oar.

The salon in the river villa had electric lights, and dinner brought from the city had been prepared for us. Mrs. Wu and Mr. and Mrs. Liu treated us with a hospitality as if we had known one another for a decade or more. They say this is the way Chinese entertain at banquets, as the two Chinese women frequently used their own chopsticks to put food on my plate. The host offered a Chinese poem, and so my husband composed a Chinese poem, Mr. Satō wrote a haiku, and I prepared a Japanese poem. The spirited Mr. and Mrs. Hayakawa translated my poem into Chinese for the two ladies.

Table service was taken care of by soldiers attached to the

warlord, which I found quite a strange experience. I felt as if I were in a scene from a barracks beyond the border that I had read about in Chinese history. Compared to the wretched previous evening we had spent in the inn in Taonan, I was overjoyed by the romantic change of surroundings. As the agreeably drunk Mr. Satō rose and began moving about as if dancing, we continued to converse. The taciturn, composed Mr. Katō seemed a bit intoxicated himself and, with his face reddening, he held a cigarette in his mouth and surveyed this scene with the gentle smile of youth. My husband, who had no capacity to drink, had quickly become drunk on the Chinese wine and repeatedly grabbed for his writing brush. Above all, Mr. Hayakawa's eloquence, full of openheartedness and goodwill, formed a core that fostered the atmosphere of a salon. A distinguished China hand, he had long maintained a friendship of sworn brothers with warlord Wu. Who knows the extent of the good fortune he has contributed in over twenty years to the relations between Japan and Manchuria-Mongolia? In the back of my mind, I was happy to see the sagacious manner in which the South Manchurian Railway Company assigned the right man to the right place. I offered my respects both to Mr. and to Mrs. Hayakawa. As a student, she had learned English at a women's school in Lüshun, and now she spoke Chinese like her husband. Such an agile disposition not only served as a wife's help to her husband but also contributed to his work. How sad it was, I thought, that Japanese women living in Manchuria were indifferent to studying the Chinese language, and I was thankful for the great preparation Mrs. Hayakawa must have undergone to master Chinese in her middle years.

When dinner was finishing, Mrs. Wu and Mrs. Liu said they wanted to show me some Chinese textiles and they accompanied me into another room. Numerous fabrics so beautiful they could startle you awake were laid out there on a table, and a salesman for the fabrics was waiting. Mrs. Wu picked out a piece and showed it to me—under the electric light, they all looked like a rainbow fluttering. "It's magnificent," I said, and Mrs. Wu replied, "Here, I'd like to give it to you. And, take this piece home with you as well," referring to the piece I had praised. I then learned that she had specially called this salesman up from the city in order to make a souvenir for me. She then took another piece, entrusted it to me, and said, "Please give this to Ms. Takenaka Shigeko in Tokyo."

We all left the villa filled with good spirit, and together with Mr. and Mrs. Hayakawa arrived back at the South Manchurian Railway office outside the city before 11:00 P.M. A Chinese meal had been prepared that evening here as well, thanks to Mrs. Hayakawa's solicitude, and although thanking her for this kindness, we just had a cup of tea. The Hayakawas and ourselves had both enjoyed the unexpectedly happy party that evening, but the time was pressing for us to catch the special train, and with no time left to query the Hayakawas about conditions in Qiqihar, we bid them a hurried farewell. When we entered the car to take us and the Hayakawas who were going to send us off at the station on the Qi-Ang line, again as guests of the warlord's wife, a corps of troops suddenly saluted us under their officer's orders. There was something quite wrong about all this, I thought, feeling my face turn flush. There wasn't a soul at the deserted station. The special train ordered by Mrs. Wu was waiting for us, and just when we were about to board it, Mrs. Wu and Mrs. Liu arrived by car to send us off. I had heard that for two women to be outside the city so late into the night was an extraordinary event, and I was again moved by their kindness. They had each brought signed photographs of themselves, which they gave to me. Sad to leave, I shook their hand, a sentimental feeling welling up within me. I thought I would never again in my life meet such people as I had here. I repeatedly said to them, "Please do make a trip to Tokyo." They had indicated a desire to visit Japan.

The train set off, and inside our compartment a neatly prepared meal of several dishes had been laid out for us, and the Chinese waiter served it with beer and tea. A military guard was placed in the corner of the room. All of this scrupulous attention must have been the work of Mrs. Wu. Aside from the locomotive, the train had only one car attached, making the rocking motion rather severe at times. By chance we repeated our experience on this special train of going from Yingkou to Dashiqiao. The moon outside the window, which we had seen that evening on the Nen River, was sinking beyond the edge of the horizon, and scattered stars could be seen in the dim sky tinged with blue. My husband said that he could understand the viewpoint of *Sai shang xing* (Travels to the Borderlands) by a poet of the Tang dynasty.

THE INN AT ANG'ANGXI

Isugi Nobutarō, the proprietor of the Angrong Hotel, had come to meet us at Ang'angxi Station. We queried Mr. Isugi and learned that a pass for the train carrying the four of us, about which he had been notified by telegram sent from the South Manchurian Railway office in Harbin that morning, had not yet been received. It should have been in the mail arriving at the station, but since it was already past 10:00 P.M., the station rule was that one couldn't open the mail. Mr. Katō, who spoke Russian well, went to bargain with the station assistant, but it was already past midnight and the stationmaster had gone home. So, when we understood that one could under no circumstances open the mail and accordingly we would be unable to change trains to the 2:56 A.M. train, we realized we had no choice but to put up in Ang'angxi for the night. I thought to myself that if we had to undergo this, it would have been nice to stay overnight in Qiqihar and get up early and tour the city quickly the next morning. In any event, the special train sent by Mrs. Wu was regrettably in vain.

The Angrong Hotel was managed by one person alone. Since there were ordinarily no Japanese guests staying there, the facilities were not terribly fastidious, but the quiet Western-style rooms in the house, which had been built by Russians, were even more comforting to us than the Japanese inn in Liaoyang. Mr. and Mrs. Isugi were frank, polite folk. Their straightforward manner of welcoming guests more than made up for the insufficiency of facilities. The chirping of crickets inside in late May together with the Milky Way visible in the sky gave me a strange feeling. Astronomical phenomena and the vapors from the earth here in the north cannot be reckoned on the basis of the seasons in Japan.

The following morning we ate aromatic Russian bread and good butter. I learned from our conversation after breakfast that Mr. Isugi, the proprietor, was a sergeant-major in the reserve cavalry and that he had been sent earlier by the army to observe Manchuria and Mongolia. He was not an ordinary inn operator, but even now seemed to be a man devoted indirectly to national affairs. He told us that he came originally from Sado Island, and we launched into a discussion of Watanabe Kohan, from Hatano village on Sado, with whom we were very close. Mr. Isugi came from the very same village as Watanabe and had, in fact, been in the same class in elementary school. This brought us closer together. We mentioned that we had recently visited Sado, and Mr. Isugi, who hadn't been back to his hometown for a long while, was only too happy to hear of recent conditions there. Surprisingly, the hotel had both thick writing paper and a brush, and, while the ink was India ink, my husband and I wrote poems as we waited for the train. We sent one to Mrs. Hayakawa in Qiqihar and left another with Mr. Isugi.

ON BOARD A TRAIN ALONG THE CHINESE EASTERN RAILWAY

We boarded the train from Ang'angxi scheduled to depart at 11:25 A.M. and headed for Harbin. Trains on the main line of the South Manchurian Railway were far better outfitted than their counterparts back in Japan, but when we boarded a train of the western line of the Chinese Eastern Railway, which had come from Europe, I sensed a certain beauty, as if the world had to a certain extent changed. The trains were now cleaner than those on this line that I had taken in 1910,[16] and the equipment was in better working order. I was quite taken aback by the train and wondered if I would even have noticed how slow my mind was working if this train were going to Europe today. The few dishes of Russian food we ordered for dinner were thoroughly satisfying. The beer that the men were drinking was German. The reason that the bill for the four of us came to about 30 yen was because of the cucumber salad we ordered. We laughed at the extravagance of this cultural dinner, compared to the 50 yuan—not even two Japanese yen—we spent to stay in the stable at Shangshiqiaozi en route to Qianshan. Yet, the view outside the window rushed over a long, dreary sandy plain. The elegant early summer garb of the handsome Europeans, men and women, who got off at each station and walked away, in particular the Russian women, in two or three minutes coming and going with the Russian architecture of the station in the background—it all made me feel as if I were seeing a movie.

FIVE DAYS IN HARBIN

We crossed a steel bridge over the Sungari River and arrived in Harbin at 8:30 P.M. on May 26. At the station we were met by Mr. and Mrs. Furusawa Kōkichi and Mr. Okabe Masayoshi of the local office of the South Manchurian Railway Company. Mr. Satō and Mr. Katō were staying at the Hoku-Man Hotel, while we—thanks to the great kindness of Mr. Furusawa, who said he would put us up in a quiet spot—were lodged at the South Manchurian Railway Residence located on a grand boulevard, which, had this been Paris, would have been the rue de Passy. I had heard that the South Manchurian Railway Residence had once been the estate of an aristocrat from the era of the Russian Empire, and it indeed was an extraordinary piece of Russian architecture with numerous rooms. Ordinarily a young man by the name of Kōno Tokimune and his wife took care of it alone, and at the time no one was staying in this immense place. Mr. and Mrs. Furusawa, who had brought us here from the station, told us to select any room in which we felt comfortable. I was greatly moved by this kindness and sensed a calm come over me as if I was staying at a mansion back in Tokyo.

I had met Mr. Furusawa once four or five years earlier in Tokyo, and I had exchanged letters with Mrs. Furusawa, but this was our first meeting. This was my husband's first encounter with either of them. Mr. Furusawa had long ago matriculated in the Russian section of the Tokyo Foreign Language School and spent many years as a diplomat in Russia. After leaving the consular life, he worked for a long stretch as director of the Harbin office of the South Manchurian Railway Company and the local Japanese Residents Association, having made contributions both in the public and the private sphere. When we met and spoke, he was not only well versed in Russian literature, but I was surprised to learn that he loved to read Japanese literature as well, even the novelists of the younger generation of writers. He was also a writer of Chinese poetry and new-style haiku. His wife, who I had heard was ill, was quite thin, but we were happy to learn that recently she seemed to have returned to good health. My intuition told me that she was a woman with a balance of elegance and intelligence. While speaking of our trip to Yingkou and after some time meeting her daughter, I felt almost moved to tears, and Mrs. Furusawa had tears in her eyes as well.

On the morning of the following day, we went with Messrs. Satō and Katō to visit Mr. Furusawa and Mr. Sakamoto Naomichi at the South Manchurian Railway office, and we also met Mr. Yagi, of the consulate, who came along. From the office roof, we saw the city of Harbin, as a lingering Mongolian wind blew and mists floated over the Sungari River beyond the city. The pure white flowers of pear trees blossomed in profusion beside a grove of elm trees near the office—this was a beauty I had never seen before. By contrast, there were only a small number of acacias, many of which I had seen in Lüshun and Dalian. Also, only a few willow catkins flew by. Most of the trees I saw were elms. Mr. Furusawa served as our guide, as we first drove along a street with numerous Russian homes on it. White Russians lived here and were now perforce subordinate to Soviet Russia. Ever since Russian and Chinese forces had been at odds, the coersion exercised by Chinese officials had become conspicuous, and White Russians were living what appeared to be much shabbier lives now. Only the mansions of Russians connected to the Chinese Eastern Railway had a breadth reminding one of the prosperous times before the Russian Revolution. There was a loneliness about these large homes and some of them were completely vacant. We saw the park that had once been managed by Russia. A row of fresh, green elms around the park had scattered elm seeds piled high in the shade of every tree. I was able to take in fully here the appearance of these elm seeds, what the Chinese poets called *yuqian*, something I loved. On benches inside the park, though, aside from young Russian men and women in groups of two or three whom we saw, all was desolation and decay. Mr. Furusawa explained that, in the era of the Russian Empire, when General Dmitri Khorvat was director-general of the railway and held control over the administrative, financial, and military rights, every evening this park would be filled with officers and their wives, lively concerts would often be held, and at General Khorvat's order the extravagance of a fountain of champagne would spew forth. We then left the city proper to visit the site of the martyrdom of Yokogawa and Oki, where a monument had been placed. At that time [of the Russo-Japanese War], Russian military camps had been in this area, and it had been a rifle range, but it was now an open field that extended far into the misty distance. Two Russian youths were waiting for Japanese who visited the monument and begging for money from them; their clothing and shoes were tattered, but their faces bespoke an innocent beauty. They had not been born beggars but seemed to be children of White Russian parents who would never return to their homeland. Perhaps I was overdrawing the tragic aspect of worker-peasant Russia.

We returned to the city and were treated to a luncheon banquet by Mr. Furusawa at the Chinese Eastern Railway Club.

As befit this place, the magnificence and gaity of the imperial period had not been lost. In several days an orchestra would be playing here every evening for one of the annual Harbin festivals, and they were making preparations in the park. June must have been spring for these people who have such a long winter here. After lunch we went to the Japanese Chamber of Commerce and paid our respects to the stone statue of Count Itō Hirobumi [1841–1909] which had been unveiled there the previous year.[17] At the time of Itō's assassination, Mr. Furusawa had come to the station as a diplomatic official to meet him, and thus he could fill us in on the real state of affairs at the time. We went also to a Japanese elementary school and were shown around the campus by its principal, Mr. Nagamoto Kiichirō. We then left Messrs. Furusawa and Satō, and along with Mr. Katō took a walk along Kitaiskaya Avenue, the grand boulevard of the city. From 3:00 P.M. until nightfall, it was alive with throngs of people, half of whom were Russians, and particularly the image of the Russian women with their gaudy early summer hats and clothing together with their white shoes formed a spectacle to be seen nowhere else in the Far East save Shanghai. The blatantly xenophobic ideas of the present head administrative official, Zhang Huanxiang, had become widespread, even to the point that signs over stores written in the Russian language were changing to Chinese, although the feel of this great avenue in its architecture, its shops, and its merchandise was that of European rusticity. Department stores of all sizes—foremost among them being the Churin Department Store—were managed principally by Russians, and Chinese shops were second to them. There was one Japanese department store that held its ground courageously, but it seemed the Japanese here were caught in a pincer by Russian and Chinese stores and couldn't stand up to the competition. One reason for this was that Zhang, using the force of his military and police authorities, had recently prohibited the use of the gold Japanese yen, which had been the only reliable currency in the northern Manchurian market since 1918. He did this to enforce in domestic and foreign transactions the ordered market in "Harbin dollars," a nonconvertible currency, which was being issued in excess with the aim of putting a squeeze on the capital holdings of the Fengtian warlords.

We next went to see the wharf by the Sungari River. Having never seen the Yangzi, this was my first experience with an immense river the size of a sea. The Sungari was probably at its greatest breadth here. Numerous boats in innumerable colors were docked there, although there were actually few Russians who had gone out to midstream. I had heard from Mr. Katō about the lively boating here in the summertime, and we had thus planned to take a motorboat to the other shore of the river, but we had to postpone this trip because of strong winds and the clouds on the open sea.

On the way home, we visited Mr. Furusawa's home and met his wife and sons. In a parlor in which the decorations and works of art softly harmonized and faintly mixed amber, jade, and cinnabar, we spoke quietly as I looked at the shimmering light from the upstairs window on half of Mrs. Furusawa's thin, innocent face like a mountain pear blossom. The feeling was not that of Harbin, in which bullying Chinese warlords swaggered about, but resembled the joy of an early summer day when I had spoken with an English lady in London before the Great War. It seems that this was due to the fact that a certain accent with roundness and strength like ivory work rang clearly in her words. That evening Mr. Katō, my husband, and I dined together at the South Manchurian Railway Residence. Mr. Satō had no time because of friends coming expressly from Fushun and he was looking into new material for poetry.

The next morning I imposed on Mr. Katō to come with me to the main Churin Department Store and other shops on Kitaiskaya Avenue to buy just a few European articles as souvenirs for my daughters. We then had lunch at the consulate at the invitation of Consul-General Yagi. In addition to Mr. Furusawa, the guests included Colonel Matsuda Kokuzō from Korea, Andō Rinzō (a military officer residing abroad), Katagiri Shigeru, Nakano Toshimitsu, and my husband and myself. Here in Harbin where the recent Chinese antiforeignism was least strong and had least attracted the world's attention, at a time when both Japan and Russia were, of course, infringing on the vested interests of the powers and their future economic incursions, I could imagine the inner diligence and maneuvering of all the people at the dinner table. For my part, I privately was unable to make up my mind on the issue of how the Japanese economy in Manchuria and Mongolia could be beneficial to both Russia and China and come to resolution without contradiction. Not only in the south, but up here in the north as well, young Chinese with an education had become awakened to the need to restore their sovereignty. While this might appear frightening from an imperialist point of view, we must congratulate the Chinese people in the name of humanity. As for men like Zhang Huanxiang, the little spoiled brat of the Chinese warlords, their baldfaced, illegal, antiforeign actions, one must assume, will provide the opportunity for this Chinese restoration. I would hope that all the Chinese military officials here use their discretion as they survey the overall situation presenting itself now.

That afternoon we went with Mr. Furusawa to see the city museum. They have assembled there quite a collection of archeological, historical, naturalist, and ethnographic materials.

Stuffed human figures depicting the lives of the Manchurian and Mongolian races, freshwater catfish and other huge fish six feet long from the Sungari River, and an animal that is recorded in the *Secret History of the Mongols*, where the name is given as *tuboshu*, were all shown for little children. We also had a glimpse of the wealth of timber and variety of animal pelts in Jilin province. My husband was looking for the primitive carved-wood writing the Oroqen people who live in the dense forests of the Amur River delta use even today when inscribing standing trees, but it was not to be found here.

When we next paid a visit to the South Manchurian Railway office, we found Mr. Katō waiting, and we parted from Mr. Furusawa and headed for the Hoku-Man Hotel. Mr. Satō joined us and we walked along Kitaiskaya Avenue, looking at the jewelry shops, furriers, department stores, children's shops, and the like. In the evening, this avenue filled up with Russians and Chinese walking along it, and at every corner Russian girls selling lilacs and irises and young Chinese selling hill haws in boiling sugar water called out to customers. There was a European flavor to the young male and female Russians sitting on benches on the sidewalk and looking out at the crowds. All the young Russian women had bobbed hair, their skirts were short, and their lighthearted gait seemed as if they were prepared at any moment to break into dance.

That evening the four of us were invited to the Furusawa home. The guests included Consul-General Yagi, Chief Librarian Kurusu Yoshisuke and his wife, and Satō Shirō, editor in chief of the *Harbin shinbun* (Harbin Newspaper). Furusawa introduced us to these people with whom we felt at home. We had a particularly delightful discussion at dinner about art. We learned as well that Mr. Furusawa wrote haiku and Chinese poetry, Consul-General Yagi wrote poems in Japanese, Mrs. Kurusu composed tanka, and that all were quite enthusiastic about it. Mr. Furusawa also said that if he could find the time, he would prepare a placard in the ancient calligraphic style of Wang Xizhi [303–61]. Mrs. Kurusu, who was young and had a jovial temperament, seemed of all the Japanese women living in China to be making the most assiduous effort to gain an agile understanding of the latest intellectual and artistic trends. Observing her frank and richly emotional nature reminded me of Mrs. Wu whom we had met in Qiqihar. Should the opportunity present itself for there to be an exchange between such women of these two countries in the area of their ideas and interests, I believe it would be of value for national understanding between the Japanese and the Chinese.

Consul-General Yagi, who seemed cheerfully inebriated, said he would like to take us that evening to a cabaret. Having never seen this form of popular amusement, Mrs. Furusawa and Mrs. Kurusu said that they would like to join us. While Messrs. Satō and Katō went elsewhere, my husband and I decided to accept Mr. Yagi's kindness. We waited until 11:00 P.M. and left Mr. Furusawa and Mr. Satō Shirō. The rest of us then got into two cars. Outside, the late night temperature was dropping quickly, and in the blowing, frigid northern wind the lights of downtown Harbin were silent, as if about to freeze. The sky was cloudy. They say that there are two representative cabarets of this city, and the one we went to had the same name as one in Paris, Folies Bergères; despite the fact that it was much smaller in scale, it still felt very dear to my heart. In a place like this one, before midnight was still early evening and the customers were still few in number; about twenty Russian dancing girls with their long arms extended from sheer, pink silk were dancing with other young women in variegated lights. Alternating with this, that evening there were vocal solos of musical selections and Russian dancing on the stage, as the rhythm shook the room. The number of patrons gradually increased, and aside from us and a group of gentlemen, everyone else was Russian. People dancing in a reddish purple haze, produced by the music, the lights, the flowers, the perfume, the odor of alcohol and tobacco all became so many male and female butterflies. Champagne cooled on ice was repeatedly poured into glasses at our table, and Mr. Yagi offered all sorts of explanations in high good humor. "This evening," he whispered, "they think that my wife is sitting at this table, so those women won't ask me to dance." Thinking it somewhat inconsiderate that no one from our table was dancing, Mr. Yagi stunned us by getting up and dancing with one of the dancing girls. I sensed that as the night progressed it was not good for Mrs. Furusawa's health, and I persuaded everyone that we should leave before it reached 2:00 A.M., when this cabaret would reach full bloom.

The next day was the 29th, and at the request of a number of Japanese living here I devoted the morning to writing poetry. That afternoon Mr. Urasaki Seiichi of the *Harbin nichinichi shinbun* (Harbin Daily News) said he would show me around, and this proved to be an opportunity to do some sightseeing. Harbin lay at the northern border of Jilin province, while the opposite shore of the Sungari River, which ran from the west northward, belonged to Heilongjiang province. After the Sino-Japanese War, it was claimed, it remained a wilderness overgrown with reeds until Russia bought up the land in the name of the Russo-Chinese Bank. The present city centers around Harbin Station, and the wharf region [Pristan] in the northwest, which faces the river, is a prospering commercial area. With Kitaiskaya Avenue, the main thoroughfare, running north-south, the numerous streets of the city laid out in a grid pattern, together with the architecture, roads, and groves of trees line up with shops in an orderly European-Russian manner. The commercial area known as Fujiadian in the northeast, facing the river, is a city with an exclusively Chinese air that the Chinese have managed for a twenty-year period, and it too is thriving. Southeast of the train station is an area of high ground known as the Xinshijie (New City), and it has become an area of rather elegant public offices, banks, and middle-class residences. The South Manchurian Railway Company office at which we were staying was located on Jilin Street in Xinshijie. To the southeast of Xinshijie, an expansive residential district known as Majiagou awaited future development, and to the southeast of Majiagou was an area of Russian residences first managed by Russia that retained the scope of luxury from the imperial period and bore the name Jiushijie (Old City). Continuing further in this direction would lead you to the vast wilderness of Jilin province. The Chinese Eastern Railway ran eastward toward Vladivostok; it also ran south to Changchun and linked up with the trunk line of the South Manchurian Railway.

It was a cloudy day with a cold northern wind blowing. On a streetcar that Urasaki, Katō, and I had boarded to go to Kitaiskaya Avenue, I tried to take out some Harbin currency to pay the conductor, and just then a sudden gust of wind blew in from the window and sent high into the sky several bills from my handbag, which I had opened. The streetcar dashed along. Everyone called out, "Oh!" but it was too late. There we were, poor travelers walking along the streets of Harbin with money literally flying about. After looking at a few Japanese and Russian shops, Mr. Katō departed, and thereafter Mr. Urasaki and I went to visit a movie theater and coffee shop. The motion picture was a saccharine American film, but it was interesting that the subtitles were written on the screen in Chinese translation. Among the viewers were far more lower-class Chinese than

Russians. The great mass of the Chinese apparently enjoyed such provocative movies full of kissing scenes. I never have the chance to go to movie theaters in Japan, and we hadn't thought we would go here; it was the first time I'd been since I was in Paris. At the coffee shop, it was the first time in twenty years that we were able to have a quiet chat with Mr. Urasaki. When he was a student in Tokyo, the young Mr. Urasaki had joined our poetry society and contributed poems to the journals *Myōjō* (Shining Star) and *Subaru* (Pleiades). I had never expected that he'd be here in Harbin. The three of us eagerly covered the ground of the past. We spoke about Mori Ōgai [1862–1922] and Ueda Bin [1874–1916], both of whom had passed away, and about old friends from the poetry society whose circumstances had now changed.[18] More than anything, we were happy to learn that Mr. Urasaki was still writing poetry. We also felt how inappropriate it was now that he should be affording us the kindness of acting as if he were our student. He remembered the names of our children and even bought some souvenirs at a Russian shop for our daughters.

Today Mr. Satō Sōnosuke set off for Changchun a day ahead of us. Because seats were unavailable on the train, we were fortunate enough to extend our stay one day and were only too happy to be able to get to know Harbin, of which we had become so fond already, even better. Politically, economically, and ethnically this international city had to be the center of the Manchurian and Mongolian enterprise, especially for Japanese; my feeling at the time was that it was a place I wanted to see more than far off California in the United States or Brazil in South America.[19]

That evening we had a splendid Japanese meal at the South Manchurian Railway Residence with Mr. and Mrs. Furusawa, and we were able to chat quietly until late into the night. The very fact that we were able to make this trip to Manchuria and Mongolia was due in large part to the good graces of Mr. Furusawa and Mr. Usami Kanji of the South Manchurian Railway Company's main office in Dalian. Thanks to the meticulous attention shown us by the Furusawas, our stay in Harbin was entirely a happy remembrance for another future day, and we thanked them for it. Mr. Furusawa and my husband were precisely the same age, and although they met for the first time during this trip, both men had been in Seoul, Korea when they were twenty-three or twenty-four years of age. Mr. Furusawa had taken up temporary residence at the Japanese legation, while my husband was at the Japanese consulate; while they ought to have seen each other frequently, they had had no interaction. Reminiscences from bygone days in Seoul were thus injected into our conversation that night. Mr. Furusawa had been much favored by Korean Legation ministers Miura [Gorō, 1847–1926] and Komura [Jutarō, 1855–1911] and thus lived in the Japanese official residence. My husband knew Mr. Komura and knew his son Kin'ichi for as long as Mr. Furusawa had. Indeed, on our present trip, Komura Kin'ichi had written letters of introduction to people in the Foreign Ministry for us. After we finished eating, the four of us wrote picture postcards to Kin'ichi and to Takahama Kyoshi [1874–1959, another writer].

From the morning of the following day, we went with Mr. Katō to make the rounds, from the Japanese consulate to the South Manchurian Railway offices, to Mr. Furusawa's home, and elsewhere, to bid everyone farewell. We then drove to the eastern suburbs of the city to take our last walk by the large Russian cemetery. We paid a visit en route to the Jile Temple built in recent years by Chinese. It was a huge temple constructed with a

Chinese style of grandeur enriched by vivid colors. Mr. Katō mentioned that many Japanese living in the area who were working for the South Manchurian Railway Company and other concerns had made contributions toward its construction. The cemetery occupied an expansive area on an open plain. A forest of elm trees offered the shade of fine fresh growth, and European-style grave stones made of marble were lined up all in white, next to each a wreath and a lamp candle offered in devotion. The scene of a multiplicity of flowers growing in front of them lacked the melancholy feel of Japanese graves and actually evoked a deeper sense of grief. Mr. Katō was fluent in Russian, and he read for us the names of the deceased from their graves and their brief stories. I felt a particular sadness at the sound of a name of a Russian woman who had died young. When we turned around, we saw a number of women here and there dressed in black wandering about among the trees with flowers in their hands. We continued to walk amid the graves a bit longer. Beneath the clear northern sky, which had become a chilly cobalt, there was no wind, no birds chirping, and the immense graveyard in the deathly quiet elm wood brought us close to the hearts of the many dead whom we had never known, as we reluctantly departed. For some reason I felt like reading a Russian novel. Photographs of most of the dead had been inlaid on the grave stones and covered by glass. Why was it that in Japan and China where we practice ancestor worship we generally show so little attention to graves? When he had worked here years before, Mr. Katō said that he frequently came to this place and read collections of Russian poetry.

After we finished lunch at the South Manchurian Railway Residence, the three of us proceeded to the station at 1:30 P.M. Mr. Furusawa, Mr. and Mrs Kurusu, Messrs. Sakamoto and Okabe of the South Manchurian Railway Company, Mr. Satō Shirō, and Mr. Urasaki, among others, came to send us off. I saw clearly that day that the style of the station's architecture had changed. The placement of the memorial to the death of Prince Itō seemed to be slightly different from what I had seen in 1912. We thanked everyone for their many kindnesses, and with the departure of the 1:55 P.M. train we bid farewell to these people and to the city of Harbin.

TO CHANGCHUN

The compartments on the Chinese Eastern Railway between Harbin and Changchun were elegant. The three of us took two rooms. Many of the passengers were Russians, and, in addition to French and Americans, we also saw Japanese on their way home from Europe via the Siberian railway. The scenery glimpsed from our window was different from that of Mongolia, much richer in greenery, giving me something of a sensation that I had returned to Japan. The land was all fertile black soil, and scattered about among green willow trees were a number of marshes, the extensions of tributaries of the Sungari River, reflecting the blue, early summer sky in a large circular basin. The boats of Chinese fishermen floated by now and again. Looking down on all this from the train window, for the first time we had a taste of the Chinese-style beauty of willow trees and water. As this spread out far to the north and east, mountain ranges of various sizes rose one above the next with an endless zone of forests and the main trunk of the Sungari, which runs for nearly fifteen hundred miles, forming a fertile zone for cultivation. As I thought about all this, I imagined that in the future northern Manchuria would probably become enormously valuable economically. At nightfall the moon appeared, and the view from our window grew even more spectacularly gentle.

We traveled 150 miles in seven hours before arriving in Changchun at 9:09 P.M. Mr. Akagi Tsuchiemon from Changchun had come to greet us one station earlier at the Kuanchengzi Station. We had established a written relationship with Mr. Akagi several years earlier. In addition to a few South Manchurian Railway Company personnel, Professor Shiratori Fumio, Mr. and Mrs. Nanbu Hōden, Mr. and Mrs. Tamura Jirō, Mr. Hamada Toyoki, Mr. and Mrs. Honjō Tokutarō with their daughter, Mr. and Mrs. Kawasaki Shigejirō, and others came to meet us at Changchun Station. That all of these people whom we have never met before should welcome us with such warmth was something we could never repay. Mr. Satō Sōnosuke who had left one day ahead of us was also there to greet us at the station. Mr. Satō was staying at Professor Shiratori's home. No sooner had we gotten out of the station than we came upon an extraordinary sight. Several dozen people were lined up on the left and right soliciting patrons to stay at the Chinese hotels; with paper lanterns bearing the name of their respective hotels in hand, they yelled out to Chinese customers leaving the station. There were actually more of these solicitors than there were customers. This is just like the practice that I have witnessed at Ise in Japan. Life needs have given rise naturally, it would seem, to the same custom.

My husband and I were led across the plaza in front of the station to the Yamato Hotel, where we stayed. When we again exchanged greetings with some people here, we learned that Mr. Nanbu of the local Honganji branch was a close friend of my husband's nephews and that both Mr. Honjō and Mr. Kawasaki were older brothers of our dear friend Kawasaki Natsuko. Mr. Honjō had lived in Changchun since just after the Russo-Japanese War and had made his fortune through his own single-minded efforts. That evening Mr. Katō went to stay at the Society Bureau of the local South Manchurian Railway office. He had worked here in the past and thus had many old friends.

JILIN

As planned, the next day we boarded a train on the Ji-Chang line at 9:00 A.M. and headed for Jilin, the capital of Jilin province. When we crossed the Yitong River and headed east, the number of mountains gradually increased and the arbor grew more luxuriant, scenery like that of Japan. It seemed as though the ancient remains of castles and temples were numerous as well. The Yinma River, a branch of the Sungari, was magnificent. In the environs of Xiajiutai Station, they had built a frontier fort in the early Qing along the 230 miles from the northern border of Jilin to the open plains of Fengtian and planted willow trees there. A section of these willows, known as *liutiaobian*, remain to this day and have become a famous site. We could see its greenery in our telescope. Mysterious peaks were interspersed among the mountains in the Tumen Range and formed a natural gate across several miles. The greenery roused me, somewhat waking my travel-weary mind. They say that fall colors offer an even more beautiful sight. In our guidebook it noted that during the reign of the Kangxi emperor [r. 1662–1722] of the Qing the spirit of rulership was strong, and they cut through to the center of this mountain range, which was the origin of the rail line along which we were now riding.

When we arrived at Jilin Station at 12:30, Nakagawa Masuzō, Kiichi Ichitarō, and Suzuki Shigekazu of the Ji-Chang Railway, Kurai Moriyuki, Okuda Ichirō, Itō Suezō, and Minehata Rōjū were all waiting for us. They were all people we were meeting for the first time. We had lunch at the station cafe, and then we followed our kind hosts, who said that they would like to show us the magnificent views of the Sungari River and the city of Jilin from the famous Mount Longtan that lies on the eastern shore of the Sungari about five miles to the north. We caught a 2:00 train on the Ji-Dun Railway and got off at Longtan Station; from the station to the foothills of the mountain, we walked about 1.3 miles along the road, although the high, narrow heels on my shoes were not fit for such a task. This took some time, and before we had even arrived at the heart of the mountain, we had to return in order to catch the next train at 3:30 and sadly gave up on our climbing. Nor unfortunately were we able to visit the pond that took its name, Longtan, from the mountain or the Longfeng Temple. The mountain was covered with verdure of fresh hazels, and nightingales were chirping on nearby branches. Mr. Satō clipped some lilies of the valley. On this two-way road, we came upon a Manchu woman who had her hair tied up in a large topknot on her head and was wearing a red floral hairpin. Perhaps this resembled the topknot mentioned in the *Wei shu:* "The women tie their hair up and make a topknot in a net."[20] The shape of the farmers' thatched houses also struck me as similar to that in Japan.

When we had hurriedly arrived in Longtan Station, we discovered that, because of an accident, it was unclear when our train would be arriving. Having finished our sightseeing in Jilin and needing to get back to Changchun, we were in a bit of a quandary. Had we known this would befall us, we would have planned to spend a night here and taken the newly opened Ji-Dun line to go to the Laoye Mountains as Mr. Usami in Dalian had encouraged us to do and relaxed during our time visiting Jilin. We had spoken with Messrs. Akagi and Honjō in Changchun about having dinner together and they were waiting for us. Mr. Katō was especially worried by this, but as if to say, "When you're up against a wall, things work out," a motor car, which Japanese from some lumber company often took from the interior, arrived en route back to Jilin. By chance good luck, these people were kind enough to allow us to ride with them. The car raced along the road at a fearful breakneck speed, an experience I never had had before. Sitting up front with my husband, Mr. Satō from time to time raised his hand and called out, "What great fun!" The reverberations and speed with which we crossed a large railroad bridge spanning the Sungari River straight as the crow flies were ghastly. We occasionally encountered Chinese walking along the road, and the men on the car would repeatedly scream warnings to them. Fortunately, we arrived at Jilin Station without incident.

From there we hired a carriage, and using up a bit of time did some sightseeing in the city of Jilin. We also climbed up midway on Bei Mountain, to the south of the city, and from there viewed the city and the Sungari. Just to the west of the station, a monument to the former warlord Meng Enyuan [1856–1933] caught our eye by the side of the road. Meng was sacrificed to Zhang Zuolin's unification of Manchuria and disappeared from the area in 1919. I heard that the unveiling ceremony for this monument was never carried out.[21] The fifteen hundred yards from the station to the eastern wall of the city had become a commercial port zone, and the Japanese consulate, the South Manchurian Railway offices, and other company buildings were located in this area. We entered the city through the Xinkai Gate, one of the eastern gates, and went directly across in a westerly direction through the bustling city. This capital city was a rich entrepôt for timber, and I had the feeling that it was quite rare to find so many residences built with log post supports and with four strong walls made of several layers of thick planks laid out laterally. We passed by a Japanese inn called the Nagoya-kan, and I thought to myself that it would have been wise to have planned to come to Jilin for one day of sightseeing and stay at this inn. Years ago Mr. Tokutomi Sohō [1863–1957] had visited this city and, like us, spent just one day here.[22]

We left the city through the Desheng Gate in the northwest and traveled about 1.3 miles further. At that point the road began to climb Bei Mountain, and on a hillock we found a tea house. Since we had no time to go as far as the Yuhuang Temple on the mountain, we did no more than take in the view from this hill. The mountain had become a park, and there were many people there that fine spring day to walk on the grass and pay their respects at the temple. From that point looking out, the Sungari River, which flowed from the Changbai Mountains to the east, bent at a point slightly upstream and went from west to east—south of the city—before moving on to the north. Facing north, the city had an irregular convex shape, surrounded on three sides by walls that faced fields and mountains; there was no wall on the south that looked out on the river. This cityscape apparently had no parallel anywhere else. The oldest name for the Sungari River appears in the *Wei shu* as *Sumo* and in the *Sui shu* (History of the Sui Dynasty) as *Sumo**, and this changed eventually to the modern Chinese name *Songhua*. Until the Zhou era [1122–221 B.C.E.], the land of Jilin that looked out on the Sungari was the stronghold for the state of Xishen (also known as Sushen); in the Han dynasty, it was the Yilou, in the Six Dynasties era the Wuji, in the Sui and Tang the Mohe, and in the Liao and Jin eras the great tribes of the Jurchens occupied this region. At the beginning of the "Treatise on Wuji" in the *Wei shu*, it reads, "The state of Wuji lies to the north of Korea. It was formerly the state of Sushen. . . . There is a great river in the land, over a mile wide, called the Sumo River." In the "Treatise on Mohe" in the *Sui shu*, we read, "Mohe lies to the north of Korea. Its communities each have chieftains and are not integrated. There are altogether seven [such communities], and one is called the Sumo*." Both seem to be referring to this region. Surrounded by mountains, Mount Liao in the southeast was particularly high. While its peak was dim, we could see a touch of blackish blue from the Changbai Mountains. There have been many older names for this range: Buxianshan and Dandandaling in the Han; Gaimadashan, Taiboshan, Tutaishan, and Taihuangshan in the Six Dynasties period; and from the Liao-Jin era it has been known as Changbaishan. The mountains near and far that we saw that day all belonged to this range, and the mountains near Jilin all had a certain gracefulness of appearance. And flowing in stark cobalt blue amid them in the form of an S, the Sungari River offered a lovely spectacle.

In the season when the river is filled with water rafts in July and August, it runs quickly, and rafts from the upper reaches float downstream. One can see the line of large lumber merchants along the wharf. In the section of the park of Bei Mountain where we were standing, the elm seeds were scattered in the shade of the fresh growth of trees forming piles here and there, and from somewhere willow catkins flew by in the air. We observed a crowd of people at one tea house; the customers were listening to a storyteller recount biographies of great heroes. The narrator was a man, and he was accompanied by a woman on a three-stringed lute. It resembled a combination of Japanese martial storytelling and the ballad drama style of *jōruri*. I was reminded of the *jōruri* enacted by Satsuma Jōun [b. 1593] and performed with shamisen; perhaps there was an influence through the Chinese storytellers who came to Nagasaki. I learned from the *Shi hua* (Essay on Poetry) of Yuan Suiyuan of the Qing that *shuoshuren* (storytellers) are similar to these storytellers and to Japanese martial storytellers. In China they use the term *shuoshu* to refer to war stories told in such texts as *Sanguo zhi* (Chronicle of the Three Kingdoms).

I thought I might like to see the Altar to the Gods of the Soil and the Grains and the Temple of Agriculture that lay outside the Donglai Gate, and several Japanese living here said that they wanted to show us Ming period writing engraved on the stone of a mountain along the river east of the city and the spirit garden with deer located at Wangji Mountain. We had no time, however, and just returned through the city to the train station, just able to catch the 5:05 train. Sadly, I was unable for lack of time to relax and chat with the people who had met us and showed us around. Our guidebook noted that Jilin was the "Kyoto of Manchuria," in the sense that it was a place of scenic beauty and ancient elegance in customs and architecture, but as a lively commercial city with timber and other products it was altogether different from Kyoto. Indeed, it would be difficult to compare the Kamo River [in Kyoto] to the might of the Sungari on which steamships and sailing vessels sailed upstream from Harbin. Also, politically this was a base of operations for the Jilin warlords, chief among them being Zhang Zuoxiang [1881–1949], and they had the might to contest the Fengtian clique of Zhang Zuolin.

BACK TO CHANGCHUN

The sun did not set for awhile after leaving Jilin, and we marveled from the train car at the scenery. The setting sun seen from the Tumen Range was extraordinarily beautiful. We arrived in Changchun at 8:40, and we proceeded to a banquet of Chinese cuisine given for us by Messrs. Akagi and Honjō at some building. I was able that evening to ask all manner of questions about contemporary conditions in Changchun. When the banquet was finished, Mr. Satō set off ahead of us on a night train for Fengtian.

The following day was June 1, and in the morning we were guided by Messrs. Akagi and Izumi Kenzō of the South Manchurian Railway Company and by foot we saw the city and suburbs of Changchun. Since the Zhou era, this area had belonged to Sushen, Fuyu, Bohai, and other states; from the Yuan [or Mongol] period, it was a grazing land for the Khorchin tribe of Inner Mongolia. In the Qianlong reign [r. 1736–95] of the Qing dynasty, a jasag by the name of Rabdan invited in farmers from Shandong to reclaim the land for agriculture; they formed a village and took the name Changchunpu (Changchun walled town). Over the subsequent one hundred years, it gradually made rapid strides forward to reach its present state of development. However, we find an early mention of the term *Changchun* in the *Liao shi* (History of the Liao Dynasty):[23] "To extend their happiness, they led an imperial expedition, and at the head of over one hundred thousand barbarian and Han troops they marched to Changchun route (*lu*)." The present city was constructed in the fifth year of the Daoguang reign of the Qing dynasty (1825); it is somewhat less than five miles in circumference, faces the left bank of the Yitong River, and forms an irregular rectangle running east-west. In getting to the city there are three hundred square miles of land straddling the station north and south that is attached to the South Manchurian Railway. This is the new city built by the Japanese. From the station plaza three major thoroughfares radiate out to the north, with large and small streets crisscrossing them and making it into a bustling European-style city. The large-scale designs were actually given the nod of approval when Gotō Shinpei [1857–1932] was president of the South Manchurian

Railway Company. Following on this, the Chinese built an expansive wharf district which also has the lively flavor of a European city. I saw a number of Japanese businesses here as well. Nihonbashi Street, which runs from the plaza in front of the train station directly to the north, links up with Beimenwai Boulevard in the wharf area. Along the way are lined up every sort of business, company, and residence—people and horse-drawn carriages blended in as if woven together. We passed by before arriving at the city's North Gate.

Fronting onto the left bank of the Yitong River, the walled city of Changchun ran roughly twenty-one hundred yards from the North Gate to the South Gate and roughly thirty-five hundred yards from the East Gate to the West Gate; its circumference was over five miles, forming, as noted, an irregular rectangle. The thin brick wall enveloping the city was a modern structure. Within the walls, one large avenue ran north-south and four ran east-west, and along them were gathered flourishing large shops and warehouses. We went to pay our respects at the temple for the city god outside the South Gate. As the shrine dedicated to the city's guardian deity, local people prayed here to famous officials and local worthies of the past who had spread morality through the region. Such temples can be seen throughout China. The image of the deity was carved in wood in such a way that the head and limbs appeared to move, something that would be rare to find in Japan. The gods of the border peoples who live in the deep forests along the shores of the Amur River are said to take the shape of mechanical effigies, and thus they were perhaps made as *yong* (wooden images), an expression that appears in Chinese texts since high antiquity. As I was thinking about the fact that Japanese *kairai* (puppets), which were transformed into the puppet theater of bunraku, emerged with the priests of the Nishinomiya Shrine in Settsu, it struck me that in the ancient native religion of Japan, as well, we have a similar god-body. Local urbanites came to worship at this temple at the three great festivals of Sanyue (third month), Zhongqiu (mid-autumn), and Dongzhi (winter solstice), and they set up a furnace to burn paper money, just as at other temples. On the walls inside this temple, the painting of an ancient, famous artist performed with technical precision was a rather poor image but, I thought, very interesting in what it was trying to depict.

Coming out through the South Gate, a long wooden bridge spanned the Yitong River. Because it was old and dangerously aslant, repair planks had been propped underneath its center so that it could continue to be used in its convex shape—quite a hideous sight. Carriage horses all forded the river rather than attempt to cross the bridge. As we went ahead and crossed, looking back over our shoulder at the river by the city wall, the loneliness of the beauty of nature that was accentuated by the heavy beams of the temple of the city god piled on top of one another pricked up our senses and was lovely.

On our way back, we saw crowds of people at the secondhand goods market (popularly known as *Xiaodaoshi* [lit. pilferers' market]) outside South Gate, again passed by the commercial wharf area, went to Kuanchengzi, the terminal station of the Chinese Eastern Railway, and walked around in the shade of tall elm trees in an expansive, quiet area on Russia Street. Mr. Katō pointed out a low, rundown Russian home on a corner of one street, and explained that it was the remains of a coffee shop where in 1918 Chinese and Japanese troops had clashed over some trivial misunderstanding that had given rise to the inauspicious event known as the Kuanchengzi incident. After the collection and distribution of goods was subsequently moved to Changchun Station, Kuanchengzi became deserted.

This tree-lined avenue, far from the throngs of people and sandstorms, lay in an area outside the city along which visitors to Changchun would inevitably roam. We unfortunately had no time to take a rest at the Chinese Eastern Railway Club that was located there. The route back made a tour through an immense park that was on the attached territory belonging to the South Manchurian Railway, and among other things we saw a waterworks reservoir there. We visited the upper-level [Japanese] girls' school in Changchun, and I had a chance to have a simple conversation with the students. The school's principal, Mr. Ōkubo Shikajirō, answered several of my questions. Although there was a Chinese-language curriculum from the third year, the students said they liked English and disliked Chinese. I thought it unfortunate that, like girls' school in Japan, classical Chinese (Kanbun) was not part of the curriculum.

We returned to the hotel, ate lunch, and that afternoon proceeded to the second floor of the Akagi Company in Hatsune-chō to do some writing. In addition to the owner, Mr. Akagi, and his wife, Messrs. Nanbu, Hamada, and Honjō arranged seating for us. Mr. Akagi led us to the viewing tower on the roof and gave us an explanation of the entire city of Changchun. Mr. Hamada had brought along to show us some of his treasured ancient Chinese pottery, while Mr. Honjō showed us some of his ancient coins, which he had been collecting for many years. That evening, thanks to the solicitude of Mr. Nanbu and Mrs. Honjō, a tea party was held at the Yamato Hotel by a group of Japanese women, and I was able to meet, albeit for only a short while, a number of these women. That night there was a lecture meeting sponsored by the South Manchurian Railway Company at the club of its Society Bureau, and my husband and I both spoke.

The following morning, before we left Changchun,

Mr. Honjō came in person to meet us, and my husband, Mr. Katō, and I went with him to his home in Hatsune-chō, a trip of some twenty minutes in all. A scroll was lying on the floor with a painting by Miss Matsuzono that I had inscribed. It was adorned as well with my colored paper and a small vertical poem card. These had been sent to him by his younger sister, Kawasaki Natsuko. We drank tea together as if we were part of a group of close friends of ten or twenty years. When we were to depart at the station, Professor Shiratori, Mr. and Mrs. Akagi, Mr. and Mrs. Nanbu, the Akagi sons, and many other women came to send us off.

GONGZHULING

We left Changchun on the 9:00 A.M. train and got off at Gongzhuling at 10:30. That day was a once-a-year athletic meet, and the stationmaster and his assistant had both gone to the park located on the South Manchurian Railway attached land where all the more important Japanese in China were gathering. We had disembarked from the train because we wanted to see the large agricultural experimentation station run by the South Manchurian Railway Company on the western edge of the attached terrain by the station. Until a carriage could be found, we walked about the Japanese city with Mr. Katō, who was familiar with the geography, and went to catch a glimpse of the park hosting the sporting event. Food in laquer boxes and sake had been brought over to a reviewing stand inside the park adorned with a Japanese-style red and white curtain, and there was a crowd such as would appear at a festival or to see a drama. Together with shots signaling the start of individual events, the sounds of cheering and applause seethed forth. All sorts of food stands were lined up, as Japanese viewers, male and female alike, dressed in their finest continued to enter the park. There were a fair number of Chinese spectators as well. My own heart throbbed seeing the happiness of these overseas Japanese who were searching for comfort in the amusement of this late spring, early summer day, their minds revived after the long winter.

When we returned to the train station, the carriage was ready for us, and we headed for the agricultural experimentation station. En route Mr. Katō pointed out that this area was under the banner of the Darkhan Wang of Inner Mongolia and that there was a grave of an imperial princess (C. *gongzhu*) of the Qing dynasty at a site about eight miles to the northwest—hence the name, Gongzhuling [lit. imperial prince range]. This princess had died of illness on her way to marry a Mongolian prince. The area had become the divide between northern and southern Manchuria. This was the highest point above sea level, and water flowing south emptied into the Liao River, whereas water flowing north poured into the Sungari.

The avenue of willow trees leading to the door to the agricultural experimentation station was magnificent. Founded in 1913, the station covered an overall area of 213 hectares; within it, 42 hectares were being used for testing crops and 165 hectares were for pasture land and for the cultivation of fodder. The experimentation station we had seen along the way in Xiongyuecheng was a branch of this one. Aimed at opening land in future in Manchuria and Mongolia, the South Manchurian Railway Company was also managing agricultural experimentation stations and farms in such places as Zhengjiatun, Fenghuangcheng, Delisi, Hailongcheng, Heishantun, Changchun, Liaoyang, Tieling, and Yanggangzi, but this site was the largest in scale. Unfortunately, every one of the many staff members was off at the athletic meet, and we were disappointed that no one was available to describe their work. We were shown around by a Chinese worker there, and we were able to observe with our own eyes. On grazing land that seemed to go on forever, we looked but couldn't see a group of sheep that were frequently the subject matter in the paintings of Mr. Mayama Kōji, an artist who worked in the main office of the South Manchurian Railway Company. We had him open a number of sheds, and we walked around looking at the various sheep. Under the character *yang* for "sheep" in Chinese dictionaries, there are many complex characters, and this was demonstrated to me in the flesh that day. In addition to Chinese and Mongolian varieties of sheep, there were foreign breeds and hybrids. They also bred many different breeds of pigs. Apart from the pasture, there was a row of large willow trees and we took a short rest in their shade. These willows also often appeared in Mayama's paintings. Looking up at the grayish blue, crystal clear sky above the grazing land and the scattered willow trees, there was a fine tranquillity as tobacco smoke fluttered up close to the three of us. The sound of firecrackers from the athletic meet were inaudible here. Japanese couples brought their children to this station and, with prepared lunches, sat on the grass a bit removed from the shade of the trees. I felt a sense of warmth at these elegant people close to the rays of the sun in the wide-open air.

While we were having a light late lunch after returning to Gongzhuling Station, Mr. Mori Tatena, whom we had met in Taonan, arrived aboard a train from Sipingjie. He had come to meet us here, and together we proceeded to Fengtian, trying our hand at composing poems. We enjoyed the kindness of Mr. Mori, who was fulfilling a promise made when we were in Taonan. And so the four of headed directly for Fengtian on the 2:04 P.M. train.

ARRIVAL IN FENGTIAN

The area south of Gongzhuling was known as the Liao River plain and is part of the Liao River delta. It covers one-fifth of the entire surface area of Fengtian province. Lying between the mountainous regions of the eastern part of southern Manchuria and western Liaodong, this massive, fertile plain extends from the northeast to the southwest as far as Shanhaiguan. Originally a Mongolian pasture, it is now well cultivated through the hard work of Han Chinese who grow soybeans, sorghum, and other grains. At the height of summer, the sorghum blocks your vision, but from our train window, as we looked out hazily over the endless green fields of sorghum only three or four inches tall, we continued to recite poems. The terrain as far as Sipingjie was new to us, and after that was land we had already crossed during this trip.

We arrived at Fengtian Station at 8:30 P.M. and were met by Mr. Kawamura Makio, director of the local Society Bureau of the South Manchurian Railway office. We put up at the Yamato Hotel in the station building. We read in the newspaper that Marshall Zhang Zuolin was steadily retreating from Beijing and that very day had left Tianjin to return to Fengtian aboard the Jing-Feng Railway. Both Chinese and high-level Japanese officials on the continent seemed preoccupied at Zhang's impending arrival. With Beijing now back in the hands of the Nationalist government, the situation was chaotic at present, and we thus had no choice but to abandon altogether our trip to the capital. After sightseeing in Fengtian, we decided to make a one-day trip the next day to visit Fushun, and then after eating we bathed and went to bed early.

Because of the steam whistles and loud noises from trains coming and going late into the night, I scarcely slept at all that night in the hotel. The next morning I arose early and wrote letters to our children in Tokyo. As I was writing I heard a faint strange noise. My husband was washing his face, and he heard it, too. We both marveled at having come to such a noisy place. Less than twenty minutes later, we noticed that suddenly people were rushing about in the station below, but we just thought that it was due to the crowds of passengers. About an hour later, Messrs. Mori and Katō, who were staying in another room, reported on an unexpected catastrophe. At a railroad overpass where the South Manchurian Railway and Jing-Feng lines crossed, as many as four cars of a train on the Jing-Feng line had been blown up. Zhang Zuolin and Heilongjiang warlord Wu Junsheng were killed, and it seemed as well that a fair number of Chinese officials and women were among the dead. They also reported that at the time of the explosion there were shots exchanged between the Japanese troops guarding the South Manchurian Railway line at the crossing and the Chinese troops watching the Jing-Feng line. We then understood what the earlier strange explosion we had heard had been, and we unconsciously frowned as a certain dreadful insight swept across our minds. Our hearts went out to Mrs. Wu, whom we had met a week earlier in Qiqihar and who, we imagined, was lamenting her loss. After breakfast until we boarded the 9:25 train on the Fushun branch line, we heard all sorts of wild rumors. These were all stories that I, as a Japanese, could not bear to hear. It seemed as though, both inside and out, the city of Fengtian was gripped with fear, the threat of danger, and chaos.

FUSHUN

After the tumult in Fengtian we caught a train as planned with Messrs. Katō and Mori. At that time a poem came to my husband's mind:

The calamity involving warlord Zhang, who crossed our path, left dust clouds in its wake.

"The South Manchurian Railway track at the crossing was blown away," said Mr. Mori. "I can't return to Sipingjie, so I'll accompany you as far as Fushun." In addition, Mr. Harada Shūzō of the general affairs section of the Fushun Coal Mines, who had come from Fushun that morning to greet us, traveled along as our guide. The train moved eastward from Yunhe Station onto the Fushun branch line, covering a distance of over 29 miles. From nearby the intermediary station of Shenjing, we were able to see, through our telescope, Dongling (the grave of Emperor Taizu of the Qing) several miles to the north.

Fushun lay on low ground some 32 miles to the northwest of Fengtian in the hills coming out to the southwest of the Changbai range. It stretched out about ten miles east to west. Its topography was said to be the result of flood waters in high antiquity amassing trees upstream at this site and creating a coal seam. A canal flowed along the contour of the hills to the north, and the Fushun Coal Mines faced the water at a 30-degree gradient on average. They were about 2.4 miles wide, covering an area of some 24 square miles. The coal seam is on average 130 feet thick—420 feet at the thickest point. Its underground deposits hold 1 billion tons of ore. The mining area is divided into several sites, which differ according to extraction methods: large pits, slant pits, large-scale strip-mining, and the like. They use all the latest equipment, including coal conveyors, coal-dressing machines, drainage machinery, ventilation, electric power, mine-fills, and lighting. The great resources of the South Manchurian Railway Company are, in fact, due largely to these coal mines, together with the railway division. More than anything else, we were stunned by the grand sight of the large-scale strip-mining in the old city of Fushun. The idea of a coal mine, which I thought were deep mine tunnels, cut horizontally and vertically into the ground to extract ore was suddenly revealed to the eye. If they just peel off a thirty- or forty-foot surface layer of oil shale, then below it is the entire layer of coal. At first, I felt that this frightful, grotesque sight was an apparition from the earth opening up its immense mouth toward the sky, but when we went down a short way and stood where stairs had been made, I sensed the magnificence of a huge open-air theater two or three times the size of those in Roman times. I felt that the human beings using nature here were like ants with intelligence. The stripped oil shale was not an extra luxury, but was dry distilled to produce crude oil. I learned that there is as well amber in the coal, and when the men in our party knocked on stone with pieces of the coal they found in the area, we often saw fine particles of star dust glittering.

The new city of Yongantai in Fushun is a European-style Japanese town managed by the South Manchurian Railway Company that recently moved because the subterranean coal fields of the old city had become a site for strip-mining coal. The architecture and roads were orderly and lovely. After a short chat with some students at the upper-level girls' school there, I had lunch with our group at the Tsukushikan in front of the school. In the afternoon we relaxed in the shade of newly grown trees in a park located in the hills rich in scenic beauty and vistas. We also walked along the left bank of the canal and looked from a distance at the city of Fushun nestled in the foothills of the opposite shore upstream. We later returned to the Tsukushikan for dinner, and afterward proceeded to an elementary school where my husband and I delivered speeches as part of an evening sponsored by the South Manchurian Railway Company. We then boarded a train, and the four of us returned to Fengtian at 11:00 P.M.

FIVE DAYS IN FENGTIAN

It was June 4. My husband and I both had come here expecting to come into contact with a certain mood, weak though it might be, and knowledge to be found in the ancient capital of a foreign land, as Kinoshita Mokutarō [1885–1945] had written in his *Shina nanboku ki* (Chronicle of China, North and South [published in 1926 by Kaizōsha]).[24] The bomb explosion that killed Zhang Zuolin, however, was about to transform the images in our minds into observations of journalistic travelers. It was awful, but we could not be indifferent and ignore it. The truth about the incident the previous morning was, for some reason, still unclear to us that day. We did not even know if Zhang was really dead, as all manner of wild rumor circulated among the Japanese, and nothing was published about it because he was carried away by car from his office in the city. There was a rumor that Chinese troops throughout the city were going to assault the Japanese city.

We went that morning with Katō to visit Ōi Jirō, bureau chief of the *Asahi shinbun* (Asahi Newspaper) branch office in Sumiyoshi-chō. We had been particularly close friends with Mr. Ōi since he was a youngster. Ōi and his staff were all busily occupied hunting down the story and gathering information in the wake of the incident, not having had so much as even a short nap the night before, they claimed. Photos from the site of the bombed train were soon to be sent by airplane, and they were hoping to make the evening edition in Ōsaka, which we were also happy to hear. Ōi was the son of an old family from Aomori, and because of relations with their stepmother, he and his elder brother Ichirō left about the same time early on for Tokyo. While working, he studied hard and had mastered English. He was full of sincerity, diligence, and agility; his nature was such that people liked him, and now he had reached his present position. He had been here earlier at the time of the incident involving Guo Songling [1883–1925], and his abilities were recognized by the home office for his filing of shrewd reports.[25] He had only just been sent by Tokyo to take up the post of bureau chief two months before. What Ōi told us about the incident diverged sharply from what our intuition was telling us from the previous day.

After leaving the *Asahi* office, we ate lunch at a nearby restaurant where we were met by Nagahama Tetsusaburō, who arrived by car. Nagahama had been a friend of two friends of ours, Chino Shōshō and Miki Taizō, from his university days. Before we left Tokyo, he had gone out of his way to give us a book and encourage us to spend some time in Fengtian. He was now serving as the dean of students at the South Manchurian Medical College run by the South Manchurian Railway Company here. We first went to visit the college. It occupied a wide area in one corner of the attached territory, replete with grand European-style buildings and offices and classrooms within. Although they accepted both Japanese and Chinese students, classes were canceled that day because of the incident the day before. We went up to the roof to take in the view, and Nagahama offered us an explanation of the local geography. From the Tang dynasty on, the Fengtian region had long been known as Shenzhou, in the Yuan as Shenyang, and from the fourteenth year of the reign of Nurhaci of the Qing it had been Fengtian.[26] To the northwest we could see the Hun River, one of the sources of the Liao River, the Japanese city located in the middle of a fertile plain that extended to the east formed a rectangle running from the northeast to the southwest in the railway's attached terrain following the South Manchurian Railway. Through the Japanese city ran two major boulevards, Naniwa and Heian, radiating directly from Fengtian Station, and large and small communities were distributed about. Here had emerged an orderly cultural city with shopping streets, rows of trees, water and sewer services, European architecture, and the like. Like the Japanese city in Changchun, though, 70 percent of the inhabitants were Chinese. A commercial wharf district (and residential area) outside Fengtian to the east half surrounded the Japanese city, taking the concave shape of a square U. This was a bustling market area with numerous Japanese and foreign shops. Further to the east was the old walled city of Fengtian. The walls were divided into an outer wall and an inner wall. The former was made of earth seven feet high and sixteen thousand meters in circumference. It surrounded the inner wall, and between the two was an expansive Chinese city in all four directions with numerous *hutong* (alleyways) off the four major avenues: North, East, South, and West. A number of gates, large and small, had been built into the outer wall, and from the roof of the college we could see directly to the west the Great Western Outer Gate. It was a clear day, and our view was unobstructed, but the heat of the sun's rays that day was quite hot. While I was drinking tea in a room downstairs, I wondered in which room Kinoshita Mokutarō, who had taught here, completed his research articles on the ringworm that infected the heads of Chinese, and I felt the great affection that I would for an older brother.

In the wake of the Zhang Zuolin incident, they were saying that it was now dangerous within the city, but thanks to Nagahama we went to visit the old walled city in a car owned by the college with a Chinese guide, Mr. Chen Yuan, who was an employee of the college and an excellent speaker of Japanese. My heart ran cold as we passed through the Japanese city at the sight of artillerymen marching while carrying field artillery pieces; at important points along the main street, the artillerymen were lying down aiming their guns, and at various sites army engineers were constructing an abatis with solid lumber. From the hotel window that morning, I had put together that they were setting up camouflage by painting trees on the planks of several train cars, and I realized that they were preparing for the unlikely event of a Chinese attack. Even now the spectacle of urban warfare seemed a gross exaggeration.

We passed through the commercial wharf area and entered the outer wall through the Great Western Outer Gate. Within the walls of the city the Chinese had promulgated martial law, and a squad of Chinese troops with bayonets attached to their guns was being led by their officer to secure the area left and right within the gate. Our car, though, passed right through without our identifying ourselves. The city inside the outer wall was flourishing, though we didn't see a single Japanese. The way Chinese along the street were gazing after us made me feel very uneasy. We then reached the Great Western Gate of the inner wall. The inner wall is constructed of black bricks; it is over three feet high, some five thousand meters in circumference, and the breadth of the wall is sufficient to plant field artillery pieces on top of it. It was built in the fifth year of the Tiancong reign of Abahai, Emperor Taizong of the Qing, or 1631. Within the Great Western Gate of the inner wall, too, there were rows of guns and bayonets shining in the light. We headed down the main street for the Great Eastern Gate, turned right at the corner of the Bureau of Finance, and paid a visit at the South Manchurian Railway office. The office building was half-Chinese and half-European in architectural design and of a grand style such that it might also have been the South Manchurian Railway Residence. Fortunately, the director of the office, Mr. Kamata Yasuke, happened to be in when we arrived.

Like Mr. Hayakawa in Qiqihar, Mr. Kamata was a well-known expert on China; and like Mr. Hayakawa, who was a sworn brother to Wu Junsheng, Mr. Kamata had sworn an oath of brotherhood with Zhang Zuolin. One could clearly see the look of sorrow and puzzlement on Mr. Kamata's face. He told us that our coming to the inner city was an act of enormous bravery: "You may not have known it, but since yesterday the Chinese walking by this gate were saying alarming, frightening things about us Japanese. For those of us who have been here for some time, this abrupt worsening of Chinese emotions has no precedent. This morning some Chinese wrote violent things on the walls of this very building, which we cleaned off immediately." His wife had evacuated the previous night by train to Dalian, and other women were retreating to the attached terrain. Thus, only male staffers were left in the office, and the Chinese employees, he said, had all left.

As Mr. Kamata was describing the scene of the previous day, when he had rushed to the site of Zhang Zuolin's death, he said that they had found several Chinese playing cards about seven-eighths of an inch wide and four inches long that had come flying out of a pants pocket and escaped the fires of the bombed train. Apparently, the party of Zhang Zuolin and Wu Junsheng had risen early and was playing cards in their train compartment. Mr. Kamata took us to the roof of the office building and pointed out the residences of Marshall Zhang and, slightly removed from it, that of Wu Junsheng. The marshall's residence where Zhang's remains now lay did not have the appearance of crowds of mourning callers, but was indeed quite desolate. The mourning had not yet begun, as the corpse was still under medical attention. Inasmuch as Wu's death was similarly being kept secret, the deaths of the two generals was still half-believed and half-doubted by Chinese and Japanese alike. Even Mr. Kamata had steered clear of making a firm statement.

Leaving the South Manchurian Railway Company offices, we drove over to Siping Street, the thriving center of the inner city, and looked over the city from the roof of Jishun Shop, which was effectively a small Mitsukoshi in Fengtian's Chinatown.[27] The imperial palace of the first two emperor of the Qing, Taizu (Nurhaci) and Taizong (Abahai), was located in the center of the inner city, and its yellowish brown bricks appeared close. In the Wensu Pavilion among these palace buildings were stored the thirty-six thousand volumes of the *Siku quanshu* (Complete Writings of the Four Treasuries). The palaces were ordinarily open for viewing, but because of the recent incident we had to pass this up. From what we had seen and according to a map of the city, the architectural style of the old city walls seemed to preserve an ancient style from the Han dynasty. Namely, the outer wall, the inner wall, and the walls of the imperial palace formed a triangular shape. The outer wall may have been an "outer fortification" in antiquity. The Jishun Shop was set up as a European-style department store. The employees of this Chinese shop received customers marvelously, to an extent surpassing that of the Japanese. I was concerned if there were clerks fluent in Japanese. It was rare in a Japanese-owned shop anywhere on the mainland for clerks to speak such a polite Chinese. It will be very discouraging for Sino-Japanese friendship and the spread of Japanese goods if we don't change our practice of belittling the Chinese people and the Chinese language.

Mr. Kamata warned us that we should leave the city and return to our hotel before sundown. I had heard that that evening we were to receive a visit from Major General Koyama Sukezō. Although we had met him in Lüshun, Guandong Army Headquarters had only late the previous month suddenly been transferred to Fengtian, and he had been transferred as commanding officer of the military police (Kenpeitai).

On the morning of the next day, the fifth, we went by horse-drawn carriage to visit Consul-General Hayashi at the Japanese Consulate. Major Giga, the military authority at the consulate and a military advisor to Zhang Zuolin, who had luckily escaped with a slight wound when the others were killed, had gathered there with several men, and they were in the midst of an important meeting. Hayashi left the meeting to come and meet us. In contrast to Mr. Kamata, he encouraged us, saying, "There's no danger—please continue sightseeing anywhere you wish." He avoided any clear reference to Zhang Zuolin's death. Seriously wounded and having lost consciousness, Zhang was taken by car to the inner recesses of his residence, and ever since then the Chinese had declined all visitors' requests for meetings, nor had he been examined by a Japanese doctor. This secret was being well preserved. On the way back, we thought of stopping to see a Muslim mosque, but we abandoned the idea in accordance with Mr. Kamata's warning. A light rain fell that evening, and it felt much like the mood set by a spring rain. As I smoked a cigarette in the hotel room, I remembered how Kinoshita Mokutarō distracted his melancholy by smelling the aroma of this tobacco on his fingertips, and these cigarettes that I'd gotten from Mr. Takai in Dalian became that much more full of emotion. A spring rain on an evening overseas and the light blue smoke of the cigarette—we could not escape the feeling that they were mixing with a certain sense of gloomy unease among Chinese and Japanese because of the incident involving Zhang Zuolin. Unrelated to the atmosphere inside or outside the city, that evening we read poetry together with Mori and Katō amid the aroma of cigarettes as a soft rain fell outside.

———■———

Thanks to Major General Koyama, the next day, the sixth, we were shown around by Sergeant Major Nishihara Toshio of the Military Police, who was not on duty. Relying on Chen Yuan from the Medical College as our interpreter, we went by a car owned by the college to visit Beiling [the grave of Emperor Taizong of the Qing]. We were making this trip on the advice of Consul-General Hayashi and thus kept it from Mr. Kamata. The tomb was outside the city, about four miles north of the train station, in a low mountain called Longye. When we crossed the South Manchurian Railway tracks en route, far off to the right we could see a famous Lama temple and to the left closer at hand was a Chinese college. This college was said to the base of operations for the local anti-Japanese students.

Trees were growing in abundance near Beiling. The outer wall of the tomb was encased in a mud-packed wall about one mile in circumference. We purchased admission tickets outside the gate and passed through an immense portal that served as an entranceway. Old pine and oak trees to the left and right of the entrance formed a dense wood, and on either side of a wide roadway large stone statues of panthers, lions, horses, camels, and elephants were either standing or sleeping. I delighted at the sight of these old Chinese graves that I had only imagined from pictures of the thirteen imperial Ming tombs. The four walls took the shape of the Chinese character *ya*, and on occasion the stone of the four corners was covered over. The staircase was made with wide pieces of jade and had fine engravings on it. Exposed to the wind and rain, it was losing its luster, and I thought it a terrible shame that people walked over it with shoes. The tomb's Longen Gate, Longen Pavilion, and the like were all constructed in the eighth year of the Chongde reign of Abahai's rule (1643). It had been refurbished many times since, as the red, yellow, vermilion, and blue coloring were vivid. In the Hall of Tablets was a treasured placard composed by the Kangxi Emperor. Behind the Longen Pavilion was the grave into which Qing Taizong's coffin had been placed and over which earth had been heaped in a mound. We climbed to the top of the inner wall—just over two feet tall—and walked around the grave's circumference. The pathway on top of the wall had a fence in the shape of a square horseshoe, and it was wide enough to set an artillery piece on it, just as had been the case on the city wall. As I was thinking about being buried in such an extraordinary place, it struck me why men of old so wanted to become sovereigns. As we went down and looked at the architecture of the buildings, the fact that a European-style chimney had been drawn on an outside column that had been touched up in recent years was less than interesting.

We returned to the stone camels and took a respite at a tea shop nearby. When we entered the door into the tomb, we had seen a sole sentry, but after that there were no other Chinese soldiers on patrol. As we were drinking the tea poured for us by the old man at the tea shop, there was a quiet loneliness without a single profane sound save the wind through the pines reverberating in the mountains. Perhaps they thought it dangerous, for there were not even any Japanese sightseers there. While relieved that, having taken this risk and come here, nothing untoward happened, we still felt almost a little disappointed.

It was then suggested that we visit the inner city, and on the way back we entered the Lesser Western Outer Gate and then the Lesser Western Gate of the inner wall. We also stopped in at the used bookshops along the alleyways outside the Great Eastern Gate. That afternoon we did some writing at the hotel, and in the evening my husband and I spoke at the South Manchurian Railway Library. Afterward we were able to send Satō Sōnosuke off; he had returned from Dalian and was headed for Korea by the late-night train. Although we had met by chance in this foreign land and traveled together for a short period of time, the locales and moods we had experienced together were both broad and deep. I felt the sadness of parting, as the Tang writer once put it, "I am off to the Xiang River [of Hunan], you to Qin." We are going to leave this place tomorrow afternoon on our way home and are about to pay a visit to Dalian and Lüshun.

BACK TO DALIAN AND LÜSHUN

We left Fengtian and returned to Dalian on June 7, putting up at the Yamato Hotel. After twenty days we were able to see our friends in Dalian to whom we had bid farewell, because we had been unable to visit Beijing because of political difficulties. We took this as a blessing and availed ourselves of the opportunity to meet and chat with these friends of ours. We also decided to visit the places we had left unseen in Dalian and Lüshun.

Our guides from the following day were primarily Nishida Inosuke and Watanabe Gen.

The day we paid our return visit to Lüshun was unlike our earlier day there. On the outward journey, we took a train and got off at Xiajiahezi Station. We strolled along a part of the Bohai beach with Nishida. It was a slightly breezy day, but the sky was clear.

In Lüshun Stationmaster Itō Shin'ichi was waiting for us. We rode off together in a horse-drawn carriage and were taken to the destroyed remains of the fort at Dongjiguan Mountain. The insides of this solid fortification, like a cavern, extended down an alley, and where you could see light flood in here and there, as if through a window, were the crumbling remains of where our forces' heavy artillery had by chance blown holes [at the time of the first Sino-Japanese War]. We did a tour around the insides, and, when we emerged, we heard the singing of a cuckoo in a pine grove not too far away that stirred all our pathos. The wind over Huangjin Mountain from the sea was getting stronger, and together with an increasingly white dense fog it blew ashore in bits and pieces against the mountain. This whole spectacle made me think of the tragic scene of lingering artillery smoke from the wartime.

When we were in Lüshun before, we enjoyed the beauty of the young acacias, and in just three weeks' time their white blossoms were in full bloom. The acacias of Huangjin Mountain were especially beautiful, like snow. In an elegant room of the Yamato Hotel at Huangjin Mountain, we smelled the aroma of these flowers and were treated to lunch by Nishida.

After lunch we relaxed for a while at Itō's official residence on the side of Baiyu Mountain, where we met his wife. In addition, a number of people among the bureaucrats of the Guandong government who wrote haiku and poetry happened to appear. Nakao Chiyoko, whom we had met in Dalian, lived here, and we were able to see her once again. Itō was the second son of Count Itō Hirobumi. We knew his elder brother Fumiyoshi, and now had the opportunity to make the acquaintance of the younger brother. A young bachelor of law, Itō Shin'ichi loved the arts to which our conversations frequently turned. One aspect of elegance from the father seemed to have been far more conveyed to this man.

After our respite, Itō put us on a small steamship at the station, and we made a tour of the harbor and a bit outside the harbor area as well. We passed by the spot where a blockader had been sunk, and he pointed it out and explained to us what had happened. A fog blown in by the wind from the open sea to the harbor grew increasingly severe, and the spaces between people standing facing one another on board the steamship became white. This was my first experience with such a stirring scene.

We made the trip back from Lüshun by bus. The level road covered with asphalt provided the stitching between the hills, and on our right we frequently saw the green of the Yellow Sea. It was extremely pleasant.

We spent a day with Watanabe Gen sightseeing throughout the city of Dalian, and while doing so we went to visit another glass factory than the one we'd seen previously. In this workshop they produced fine cut glass, and they were now primarily making utility items for the Chinese. We visited the South Manchurian Railway Library and had the pleasure of getting to know Professor Matsuzaki Tsuruo. Another day we were joined by Nishida, Katō, Watanabe, and Mori Tatena, who had come from Sipingjie to convene a tanka party in a room of the Yamato Hotel.

In the evening we sponsored a tanka party together with a group of poets from Dalian at a pavilion of the Hoshigaura. And so we spent five nights in Dalian, and on the twelfth [of June] we boarded the *Amerikamaru*, the same ship that had brought us here for the trip home. Many people came to send us off at the pier. Among them were Mrs. Usami, Mrs. Kohiyama, and Mrs. Ishikawa, Mr. Katō, with whom we had traveled in Manchuria and Mongolia, and Nishida Inosuke, who had been so terribly kind to us, like a brother, during our stay in Dalian. Parting was painful.

THE ROAD HOME

We happened to be on board the same ship as Mr. Kōmuchi Tsunetaka, a director of the South Manchurian Railway Company, and Mr. Fukazawa Noboru of the Harbin Lumber Company. Mr. Kōmuchi was a distant relative from the same hometown as my husband, although they had never met before. The sea route was calm. Kano Sōsaburō of Fukuoka sent us a wireless communication to the ship, encouraging us to pay a visit on our way home to the Kansuijō, a new residence outside the city of Fukuoka, but since we hadn't been able to go to Beijing, I wanted to return as quickly as we could to Tokyo. We turned down his kind offer and proceeded directly for Kōbe. We then overnighted in Kyoto, arriving back in Tokyo on the morning of June 17. The weather seemed different, as the acacia blossoms in our home in the suburbs had all fallen about in disorder.

NOTES

YOSANO AKIKO AND HER CHINA TRAVELOGUE OF 1928

1. I describe their writings in chapter 9 of my book, *The Literature of Travel in the Japanese Rediscovery of China, 1862–1945* (Stanford: Stanford University Press, 1996).

TRAVELS IN MANCHURIA AND MANGOLIA

Man-Mō yūki. What follows is a translation of the travel narrative of Yosano Akiko, subtitled "Kinshū ihoku no ki" (Account of Jinzhou and points north), which is included together with a collection of her poems and those of her husband, Yosano Tekkan (Hiroshi, 1873–1935), from their 1928 trip.

1. Yosano Akiko lost her younger brother in the fighting of the first Sino-Japanese War of 1894–95. She later composed what has since become a widely celebrated poem in his honor, memorized by generations of Japanese school children.

2. A *pipa* is a Chinese string instrument resembling a lute. It has

a fingerboard with frets. A *qin* is a Chinese instrument resembling a zither.

3. When in late April 1928 the troops of Generalissimo Jiang Jieshi (Chiang Kai-shek, 1887–1975) entered the city of Jinan to administer the coup de grâce to Manchurian warlord Zhang Zuolin and complete the Northern Expedition, the Japan government dispatched five thousand troops to protect their two thousand nationals resident there and their property. Fighting erupted in early May with vicious atrocities reported on both sides, and Jiang was forced to retreat.

4. By Sima Qian (135?–93 B.C.E.), the great progenitor of Chinese historiography, 130 fascicles.

5. Ōmachi was a poet and literary scholar who visited northeast China in 1915–16; Tayama was a writer and poet as well who visited Manchuria in 1923. Both wrote travel accounts. A novelist and painter, Arishima was also the younger brother of the writer Arishima Takeo (1878–1923) and the older brother of writer Satomi Ton (1888–1983). Masamune was a painter and author and the younger brother of the great writer Masamune Hakuchō (1879–1962).

6. The *Huainanzi,* in twenty-one fascicles, is a work prepared on the orders of Liu An (179–122 B.C.E.), the prince of Huainan and grandson of Liu Bang (256–195 B.C.E.), founder of the Han dynasty. It generally reflects a Daoist predilection.

7. One of the standard dynastic histories, written by Wei Shou (506–72) of the Northern Qi dynasty, in 140 fascicles. The Northern Wei lasted from 386 to 534.

8. The acclaimed writer who had visited China several years earlier and died in the year prior to Yosano's trip. His China travelogue has been translated into English by Paul Scott as *Shanghai Friends,* in *Japanese Travelogues of China in the 1920s: The Accounts of Akutagawa Ryūnosuke and Tanizaki Jun'ichirō,* ed. Joshua A. Fogel, special issue of *Chinese Studies in History* 30.4 (Summer 1997), pp. 71–103.

9. One of the founders of modern anthropology in Japan, Torii was a professor at Tokyo Imperial University and lived in Manchuria, Mongolia, and southwest China during field trips in the early

years of the twentieth century. His travelogue of Mongolia is mentioned by Yosano below.

10. And, since 1945, once again called Shenyang.

11. Zhang Zuolin was a warlord of the larger Manchurian region who was seen for a time as being in Japanese pay. That courtship was now over, as Yosano would soon discover.

12. See note 2 above.

13. These are the measurements, converted into Western feet and yards, that Yosano gives, but they do not work. My suspicion is that the circumference figure is too small.

14. Although he never taught at a university, Naka Michiyo is generally considered one of the founding figures of modern Japanese sinology. In the late nineteenth century he wrote a six-volume history of China, entitled *Shina tsūshi* (Comprehensive History of China), in literary Chinese, a work that circulated in China as well.

15. One of many local temples dedicated to Guandi, China's god of warfare, based on a historical personage of the late second and early third centuries C.E.

16. I think this is an error for 1912.

17. The great diplomat and political leader of the Meiji period (1868–1912), Itō was assassinated by an angry Korean nationalist, on the eve of Japan's annexation of Korea, in front of the Harbin railway station.

18. Both Mori and Ueda were famed writers and critics primarily of the Meiji era.

19. Both of these places also had substantial immigrant Japanese populations.

20. See note 5 above.

21. Yosano strongly suggests that Meng Enyuan was killed in 1919 and thus a monument had been built to him. In fact, he escaped to his native Tianjin and was alive at the time of her travels in the Northeast.

22. Famed critic and journalist of the Meiji and Taishō eras (1912–26) who wrote prolifically.

NOTES

23. Another of the official standard histories, this history of the Liao (or Khitan) era runs to 106 fascicles. It was the work of Tuo-ke-tuo and others of the Yuan period.

24. Kinoshita was a poet and a medical doctor who went to China in October 1916 to teach at the South Manchurian Medical College in Fengtian. He remained on the mainland for four years. *Shina nanboku ki* is his account of those years in China. See Joshua A. Fogel, *The Literature of Travel in the Japanese Rediscovery of China, 1862–1945* (Stanford: Stanford University Press, 1996), pp. 157–58.

25. An incident in which Chinese militarist Guo Songling switched sides in the local warlord politics, joined forces with Feng Yuxiang (1882–1948), and attacked Zhang Zuolin. He was himself attacked and killed by Japanese forces on December 24, 1925, en route back to Shenyang.

26. There is some sort of error here, either Yosano's or a typographical one. This emperor died in the ninth year of his reign.

27. Mitsukoshi was and still is a well-known department store chain throughout Japan and abroad, a fact known to all of Yosano's Japanese readers.

GLOSSARY

Adachi Nagako　足立永子
Ai　靉
Aikawa　相川
Akagi Tsuchiemon　赤木槌右衛門
Akutagawa Ryūnosuke　芥川龍之介
Amerikamaru　アメリカ丸
Andong　安東
Andō Rinzō　安藤鱗三
An-Feng　安奉
Ang'angxi　昂昂溪
Angrong　昂榮
Anshan　鞍山
Aomori　青森
Arishima Ikuma　有島生馬
Arishima Takeo　有島武郎
Atomi　跡視
Awano Shun'ichi　粟野俊一
Baitou　白頭
Baiyu　白玉
Bamiancheng　八面城

bao 包

Baotai 寶臺

Bayantaria 白音太拉

Bei 北

Beiling 北陵

Beimenwai 北門外

Benxi 本溪

Bixiao 避霄

Bo 博

Bohai 渤海

Bungei kurabu 文藝俱樂部

Bunka Gakuin 文化學院

bunraku 文樂

Buxianshan 不咸山

Caitie 採鐵

Chai 柴

Chakhar 察哈爾

Changbai 長白

Changchun 長春

Changchunpu 長春堡

Changjin 長津

Changtu 昌圖

Changtuxian 昌圖縣

chending 沈丁

cheng 城

Chen Xingya 陳興亞

Chen Yuan 陳源

Chingisu kan jitsuroku 成吉思汗實錄

Chino Shōshō 茅野蕭蕭

Chongde 崇德

Ciqing 慈清

Ciyun 慈雲

Congjun xing 從軍行

Da'an 大安

Dajiang 大江

Dalian　大連
Daliang　大梁
Dandandaling　單單大嶺
Daoguang　道光
Darkhan Wang　達爾罕王
Dashiqiao　大石橋
Datong　大通
Delisi　得利寺
Desheng　德勝
dingzihua　丁子花
Dongjiguan　東雞冠
Donglai　東萊
Dongling　東陵
Dongping　東屏
Dongzhi　冬至
Du'erbodu (Dörbed)　杜爾伯都
Fenghuangcheng　鳳凰城
Fengtian　奉天
Feng Yuxiang　馮玉祥
Fu-hui　福會
Fujiadian　傅家甸
Fujiyama Kazuo　藤山一男
Fukazawa Noboru　深澤暹
Fukuoka　福岡
Fukushō kakō　福昌華工
Fumiyoshi　文吉
Furusawa　古澤
Furusawa Kōkichi　古澤幸吉
Furuyama Katsuo　古山勝男
Fushun　撫順
Futabatei Shimei　二葉亭四迷
Fuyu　扶餘
Gaimadashan　蓋馬大山
Ganquanpu　甘泉堡
Giga　義峨

gongzhu 公主
Gongzhuling 公主嶺
Gotō Shinpei 後藤新平
Guandi 關帝
Guangyou 廣祐
Guihua cheng Tümed 歸化城土默特
güng (gong) 公
Guo'erluosi (Gorlos) 郭爾羅斯
Guo Songling 郭松齡
Hailongcheng 海龍城
Haiyun 海雲
Hamada Toyoki 濱田豐樹
Han 漢
Han shu 漢書
Harada Shūzō 原田周藏
Harbin 哈爾賓
Harbin shinbun 哈爾賓新聞
Harbin nichinichi shinbun 哈爾賓日日新聞
Hatano 畑野
Hatsune-chō 初音町
Hayakawa 早川
Hayakawa Masao 早川正雄
Hayashi 林
Heian 平安
Heilongjiang 黑龍江
Heishantun 黑山屯
Higashi Mōko 東蒙古
Hoku-Man 北滿
Honganji 本願寺
Hongwu 洪武
Honjō Tokutarō 本城德太郎
Hōryūji 法隆寺
Hoshigaura 星ケ浦
Huainanzi 淮南子
huamancao 華鬘草

Huangjin　黃金
Hun　渾
Huoliansai　火連塞
hutong　胡同
Ichirō　一郎
Ise　伊勢
Ishikawa　石川
Isugi Nobutarō　井杉延太郎
Itō Hirobumi　伊藤博文
Itō Shin'ichi　伊藤眞一
Itō Suezō　伊東季藏
Izumi Kenzō　泉顯藏
Jiang Jieshi (Chiang Kai-shek)　蔣介石
Ji-Chang　吉長
Ji-Dun　吉敦
Jile　極樂
Jilin　吉林
Jin　金
Jingde　景德
Jing-Feng　京奉
Jin'gang jing rushuo zhu　金剛經如説注
Jingping　淨瓶
Jinli　金利
Jinyin'gang　金銀崗
Jinzhou　金州
Jishun　吉順
Jiugong　九宮
Jiuliancheng　九連城
Jiushijie　舊市街
jōruri　淨瑠璃
kairai　傀儡
Kaiyuan　開原
Kaizōsha　改造社
Kamata Yasuke　鎌田彌助
Kamo　鴨

Kangxi　康熙

Kano Sōsaburō　加野宗三郎

Kansuijō　環水莊

Katagiri Shigeru　片桐茂

Katō Ikuya　加藤郁哉

Kawahigashi Hekigotō　河東碧梧桐

Kawamura Makio　河村牧男

Kawasaki Natsuko　河崎夏子

Kawasaki Shigejirō　河崎繁次郎

Kenpeitai　憲兵隊

ki　キ

Kiichi Ichitarō　私市一太郎

Kin'ichi　欣一

Kinoshita Mokutarō　木下杢太郎

"Kinshū ihoku no ki"　金州以北の記

Kōan　弘安

Koguryŏ　高句麗

Kohiyama　小日山

Kōmuchi Tsunetaka　神鞭常孝

Komura Jutarō　小村壽太郎

Kōno Tokimune　河野時宗

Koyama Sukezō　小山介藏

Kuanchengzi　寬城子

Kurai Moriyuki　倉井盛行

Kurusu Yoshisuke　來栖義助

Laoye　老爺

lianhua shuangjing　蓮花雙井

Liao　遼

Liaodong　遼東

Liaodong wenxian zhenglüe　遼東文獻徵略

Liao shi　遼史

Liaoyang　遼陽

Liaoyuan　遼源

Li　李

Li Bo　李白

Liu An　劉安
Liu Bang　劉邦
Liu Bingzao　劉炳藻
Liu Dequan　劉得權
Liu Tailin　劉太琳
liutiaobian　柳條邊
liuxu　柳絮
Longen　隆恩
Longfeng　龍鳳
Longqing　隆慶
Longquan　龍泉
Longshou　龍首
Longtan　龍潭
Longye　隆業
lu　路
Lüshun　旅順
Ma　馬
Majiagou　馬家溝
Man-Mō yūki　滿蒙遊記
mantou　饅頭
Man'yōshū　萬葉集
Manzhouli　滿洲里
Masamune Hakuchō　正宗白鳥
Masamune Tokusaburō　正宗的三郎
Matsuda Kokuzō　松田國三
Matsue　松江
Matsuzaki Tsuruo　松崎鶴雄
Mayama　眞山
Mayama Kōji　眞山孝治
meng　盟
Meng Enyuan　孟恩遠
mianxian　面鹹
miao　廟
Miki Taizō　三樹退三
Minehata Rōjū　峰旗良充

Mitsukoshi　三越

Miura Gorō　三浦梧樓

Mizhen　迷鎮

Modaoshi　磨刀石

Mohe　靺鞨

Mōko ryokō　蒙古旅行

Moliugen (Mergen)　墨留根

Morinaga　森永

Mori Ōgai　森鷗外

Mori Tatena　森立名

Muling　穆陵

Muzong　穆宗

Myōgi　妙義

Myōjō　明星

Nagahama Tetsusaburō　長濱哲三郎

Nagamoto Kiichirō　永元喜一郎

Nagoya-kan　名古屋館

Naitō Taisuke　內藤碓介

Nakagawa Masuzō　中川增藏

Naka Michiyo　那珂通世

Nakamura Shin　中村信

Nakano Toshimitsu　中野英光

Nakao Chiyoko　中尾千代子

Nanbu Hōden　南部法電

Naniwa　浪華

Nanshan　南山

Nanshan'gou　南山溝

Natsume Sōseki　夏目漱石

Nen　嫩

Niangniang　娘娘

Nihonbashi　日本橋

Nishida　西田

Nishida Inosuke　西田猪之輔

Nishihara Toshio　西原登志夫

Nishimura Kiyoshi　西村潔

Nishinomiya　西宮
Niuxintai　牛心臺
obo　鄂博
Ōi Jirō　大井二郎
Okabe Masayoshi　岡部正義
Okada Ken'ichi　岡田兼一
Ōkawa　大川
Oki　沖
Ōkubo Shikajirō　大久保鹿次郎
Okuda Ichirō　奥田一郎
Ōkura　大倉
Ōmachi Keigetsu　大町桂月
Ōta Hidejirō　太田秀次郎
pingfang　平房
popoding　婆婆丁
Pu'an　普安
Puji　普濟
qi　旗
Qi　齊
Qiandingshan　千頂山
Qi-Ang　齊昂
qianglang　蜣螂
Qianhuashan　千華山
Qianlong　乾隆
Qianshan　千山
Qianshan youji　千山遊記
Qiaotou　橋頭
Qin　秦
Qiongxiao　瓊霄
Qiqihar　齊齊哈爾
Rabdan　拉布坦
Sado　佐渡
Sai shang xing　塞上行
Saishoku to rōdō mondai　菜食と勞働問題
Sakamoto Naomichi　坂本直道

Sanguo zhi 三國誌
Sanjiangkou 三江口
Sanmiancheng 三面城
Sansi 三四
Sanyue 三月
Satō Shirō 佐藤四郎
Satō Sōnosuke 佐藤惣之介
Satsuma Jōun 薩摩淨雲
Seitō 青鞜
Settsu 攝津
Sha 沙
shahe 沙河
Shahezhen 沙河鎮
shajijie maotu (shaajagai modu) 沙雞街茅土
Shangshiqiaozi 上石橋子
Shanhaiguan 山海關
Shenjing 深井
Shenyang 瀋陽
Shenzhou 瀋州
Shiguan 十觀
Shi hua 詩話
Shiji 史記
Shina nanboku ki 支那南北記
Shina tsūshi 支那通史
Shiratori Fumio 白鳥文雄
Shi Yuheng 施豫恒
Shuangliuzhen 雙流鎮
Shunzhi 順治
shuoshu 説書
shuoshuren 説書人
si 寺
Si'an 四庵
Siku quanshu 四庫全書
Sima Qian 司馬遷
Sinŭiju 新義州

Siping 四平
Sipingjie 四平街
Si-Tao 四洮
sōdachi 曹達地
Songhua 松花
Subaru スバル
Sugimoto Shunki 杉本春喜
Sui shu 隋書
Sujiatun 蘇家屯
Sukegawa Tokuhai 助川德軰
Sumida 隅田
Sumiyoshi-chō 住吉町
Sumo 速末
Sumo* 粟末
Su Qin 蘇秦
Sushen 肅愼
Suzuki Shigekazu 鈴木重一
Tai 泰
Taiboshan 太白山
Taigushan 太孤山
Taihe 太和
Taihuangshan 太皇山
taiji 台吉
Taizi 太子
Taizong 太宗
Taizu 太祖
Takahama Kyoshi 高濱虛子
Takai 高井
Takenaka Shigeko 竹中繁子
Tamura Jirō 田村次郎
Tang 唐
Tanggangzi 湯崗子
Tanghe 湯河
Tanizaki Jun'ichirō 谷崎潤一郎
tanka 短歌

Tao-Ang　洮昂
Taor　洮兒, 洮留, 洮爾
Taonan　洮南
Tayama Katai　田山花袋
Tenshō　天正
Tiancong　天聰
Tianming　天命
Tianqi　天齊
Tieling　鐵嶺
Tokutomi Sohō　德富蘇峰
Tōkyō asahi shinbun　東京朝日新聞
Tongjunting　統軍亭
Tongliao　通遼
Torii [Ryūzō]　鳥居龍藏
Tsukushikan　筑紫館
tuboshu　土撥鼠
Tuguhun　吐谷渾
Tushan　禿山
Tumen　土們
Tuo-ke-tuo　托克托
Tutaishan　徒太山
Ueda Bin　上田敏
Uenaka　植半
Umehara Shūji　梅原秀次
Urasaki Seiichi　浦崎成一
Usami　宇佐美
Usami Kanji　宇佐美寬爾
Wakabayashi Hyōkichi　若林兵吉
wang　王
Wang Changling　王昌齡
Wang'ershan　望兒山
Wangji　望祭
Wangxiaoshan　望小山
Wang Xizhi　王羲之
Watanabe Gen　渡邊嚴

Watanabe Kohan　渡邊湖畔
Wei　魏
weique　葦雀
Wei Shou　魏收
Weishu　魏書
Wensu　文溯
Wufo　五佛
Wuji　勿吉
Wujing　無景
Wu Junsheng　吳俊陞
Wulongbei　五龍背
Wulongge　五龍閣
Wusi　五寺
Wu Rong　吳融
Xi　細
Xiajiahezi　夏家河子
Xiajiutai　下九臺
Xianbi　鮮卑
xianren biansuo　仙人便所
Xiang　湘
"Xiangping cheng"　襄平城
Xiangyan　香嚴
Xiao　瀟
Xiaodaoshi　小盜市
Xiaoliang　小梁
Xiashiqiaozi　下石橋子
Xing'an　興安
Xinkai　新開
Xinshijie　新市街
Xiongyuecheng　熊岳城
Xishen　息慎
Xuchuan　虛川
Xue'an　雪庵
ya　亞
Yagi　八木

Yalu　鴨綠

Yamamoto Ken'ichi　山本憲一

Yamato　大和

yang　羊

yanghua　楊花

yanzihua　燕子花

yanziyi　燕子翼

Yilehuli　伊勒呼里

Yilou　挹婁

Yingkou　營口

Yingzikou　營子口

Yinma　飲馬

Yitong　伊通

Yokogawa　橫川

yong　俑

Yongantai　永安臺

Yosano Akiko　與謝野晶子

Yosano Tekkan (Hiroshi)　與謝野鐵幹 (寬)

Yoshida　吉田

Yoshii Yū　吉井勇

You Qianshan ji　遊千山記

Yuan　元

Yuanbao　元寶

Yuanchao bishi　元朝祕史

Yuan Suiyuan　袁隨園

Yuantong　圓通

Yu Chonghan　于沖漢

Yuguan　渝關

Yuhuang　玉皇

Yunhe　運河

Yunxi　雲棲

Yunxiao　雲霄

yuqian　榆錢

Zhalaite (Jalaid)　札賚特

Zhang Huanxiang　張煥相

Zhangtaizi　張臺子

Zhang Wenzhen　張文貞

Zhang Xueliang　張學良

Zhang Zemin　張則民

Zhang Zuolin　張作霖

Zhang Zuoxiang　張作相

zhasake (*jasag*)　札薩克

Zhengjiatun　鄭家屯

Zhenhaiying　鎮海營

Zhenjiang　鎮江

Zhennanpu　鎮南浦

Zhifu　芝罘

Zhonghui　中會

Zhongqiu　中秋

Zhou　周

zidingxiang　紫丁香

zongzi　粽子

Zuyue　祖越

INDEX